THE AMERICAN BOY'S HANDY BOOK

THE AMERICAN BOY'S HANDY BOOK

This abridged version of *The American Boy's Handy Book*, originally published by Charles Scribner's Sons in 1882, is published by:
ULYSSES PRESS
P.O. Box 3440
Berkeley, CA 94703
www.ulyssespress.com

ISBN10: 1-56975-686-4
ISBN13: 978-1-56975-686-7
Library of Congress Control Number 2008904140

Editorial and Production: Lauren Harrison, Tamara Kowalski,
   Elyce Petker, Emma Silvers
Cover design: Double R Design
Interior design and layout: what!design @ whatweb.com

Printed in Canada by Transcontinental Printing
10 9 8 7 6 5 4 3 2 1

Distributed by Publishers Group West

CONTENTS

Preface   **xiii**

Part I · The Boy Camper

Chapter 1 · Knots Bends & Hitches   **2**

➻ How To Make a Horse-Hair Watch-Guard   5
➻ Miscellaneous   6

Chapter 2 · How to Camp Out Without a Tent   **14**

➻ The Rustic Cottage   16
➻ Hints to Amateur Campers   23

Chapter 3 · Snow Houses   **26**

Part II · The Boy Boater

Chapter 4 · Home-Made Boats   **30**

➻ Birth of the "Man-Friday" Catamaran   31
➻ The Crusoe Raft   33
➻ Slab Canoe   35
➻ Indian Birch Bark Canoe   38
➻ A Canvas Canoe   49

Torch

BOAT
Leg-of-mutton Rig

➤ The Dug-out	50
➤ How to Build a Siwash Canoe	50
➤ The Scow	51
➤ A Floating Camp, or the Boy's Own Flat-Boat	55
➤ The Yankee Pine	60

Chapter 5 • How to Rig and Sail Small Boats — **64**

➤ How to Sail a Boat	65
➤ Simplest Rig Possible	68
➤ Leg-of-Mutton Rig	69
➤ The Latteen Rig	71
➤ The Cat-Rig	72
➤ How to Make a Sail	72
➤ Hints to Beginners	73

Chapter 6 • How to Make the Tom Thumb Ice-Boat and Larger Craft — **76**

Part III • The Boy Fisherman

Chapter 7 • Home-Made Fishing Tackle — **82**

➤ The Rod	83
➤ Tin and Spool Reel	84
➤ The Forked-Stick Reel	85
➤ Home-Made Nets	85
➤ A Home-Made Minnow Bucket	88
➤ Inhabitants of the Water	88

Chapter 8 • Novel Modes of Fishing — **90**

➤ The Pistol Reporter	91
➤ The Floating Tip-Up	92
➤ The Bell Pole	92
➤ "Jugging for Cats"	93
➤ The Dancing Fisherman	95
➤ Toy Boats for Fishing	95

➼ The Wooden Otter 96
➼ Fishing for Fresh-Water Clams 96

Chapter 9 · Dredge Tangle and Trawl Fishing **98**

➼ The Tangle 100
➼ The Trawl 100
➼ How to Make a Bake-Pan Dredge 101
➼ A Tin-Pail Dredge 102
➼ How to Make a Broomstick Tangle 102
➼ The Old Chain Tangle 103
➼ Hints and Suggestions to Amateurs 103
➼ The Use of the Tangle 105

Chapter 10 · Winter Fishing **106**

➼ Smelt Fishing and the Smelt Fisher's House 108
➼ The Spearsman's Shanty 110
➼ Snaring Fish 111
➼ Spearing Fish 112
➼ How to Build a Fishing House 113

Part IV · The Boy Hunter

Chapter 11 · Home-Made Hunting Apparatus, Etc. **116**

➼ Archery 118
➼ The Buckeye Bow 119
➼ Spearing Fish 120
➼ How to Make a Fish Spear 121
➼ How to Make the Torches and Jack-Lights 122
➼ Whittling 122
➼ The Elastic Gun 123
➼ The Boomerang 124
➼ The Whip-Bow 127
➼ Throw-Sticks 129

»+ The Bird-Bolas   129
»+ The Elastic Cross-Bow (A New Kind of Cross-Bow)   130

Chapter 12 · How to Make Blow-Guns
Elder Guns, Etc.   **132**

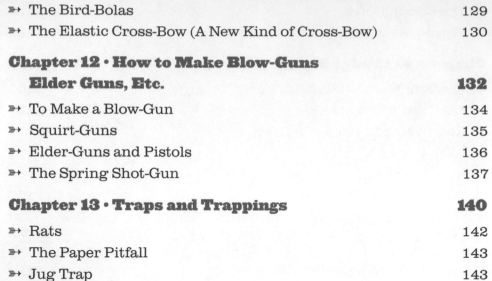

»+ To Make a Blow-Gun   134
»+ Squirt-Guns   135
»+ Elder-Guns and Pistols   136
»+ The Spring Shot-Gun   137

Chapter 13 · Traps and Trappings   **140**

»+ Rats   142
»+ The Paper Pitfall   143
»+ Jug Trap   143
»+ The Mole and How to Trap Him   144
»+ The Figure Four   145
»+ Mole Trap   145
»+ The Toll-gate Trap   146
»+ The Partridge Snare   148
»+ Set-Line Snares   148
»+ The Spring Snare   149
»+ Hen-Coop Trap   150

Chapter 14 · Decoys   **152**

»+ Dead Duck Decoys   154
»+ Shingle Snipe and Plover Decoys   155

Part V · The Boy Inventor

Chapter 15 · Bird Singers Music and Noise Makers   **158**

»+ The Block Bird Singer   159
»+ The Corn-stalk Fiddle   160
»+ The Pumpkin-vine Fife   161
»+ A Pumpkin-vine Flute   161
»+ The Voice Disguiser   161

꩜ The Locust Singer   162
꩜ How to Make an "Uncle Enos" Banjo   163

Chapter 16 · The Water-Telescope   166
꩜ How to Make a Wooden Water-Telescope   167
꩜ A Tin Water-Telescope   168

Chapter 17 · Fourth of July Balloons with New and Novel Attachments   170
꩜ How to Make a Fourth of July Balloon   171
꩜ Balloons with Parachutes   176
꩜ Paper Fire-works   179
꩜ Paper Thunderbolts   179
꩜ The Fuse   180
꩜ Parachutes   180

Chapter 18 · How to Make a Magic Lantern, A Kaleidoscope   182
꩜ A Home-made Magic Lantern   183
꩜ A Home-made Kaleidoscope   185

Chapter 19 · How to Make Various and Divers Whirligigs   186
꩜ Potato Mill   187
꩜ A Saw-Mill   188
꩜ The Rainbow Whirligig   189
꩜ A Paradoxical Whirligig   191
꩜ The Phantasmoscope, or Magic Wheel   191

Chapter 20 · The Universe in a Card-Box   194

Part VI · The Boy Naturalist

Chapter 21 · How to Stock, Make, and Keep a Fresh-Water Aquarium — 200

➻ Aquariums — 201
➻ The Frog — 208

Chapter 22 · How to Stock, Make, and Keep a Marine Aquarium — 210

Chapter 23 · How to Collect for a Marine Aquarium — 216

Chapter 24 · Dogs — 220

➻ What They are Good For and How to Train Them — 221
➻ How to Choose a Dog — 221
➻ How to Train Dogs — 223
➻ To Teach a Dog to Retrieve — 225
➻ Pointers and Setters — 225
➻ Pet Dogs — 226

Chapter 25 · Insects — 230

➻ Preserving Insects — 231
➻ Morse Insect Box — 232
➻ The Lawrence Breeding Box — 232
➻ Spiders — 233
➻ How to Make Beautiful or Comical Groups and Designs of Insects — 234

Part VI · The Boy Gamer

Chapter 26 · Kite Time — 238

➻ Man Kite — 240
➻ A Boy Kite — 244
➻ Frog Kite — 244
➻ The Butterfly Kite — 245

The King Crab Kite 246
Fish Kite 246
The Turtle Kite 247
The Shield Kite 248
A Star Kite 248
The Chinese Dragon Kite 249
The Japanese Square Kite 250
The Moving Star 250
Biggest Kite on Record 251
Thousand Of Kites 251
The Tailless Kite—Holland Kite 252

Chapter 27 · War Kites 254

Unarmed War Kite 255
Armed Kites 256
Armed Kite Fighting 257
Kite Clubs 258

Chapter 28 · Snowball Warfare ... 260

How to Build Snow-Forts 262
How to Make an Ammunition Sled ... 263
Rules of the Game 265
A Snow Battle 266
How to Bind a Prisoner Without a Cord ... 269
Company Rest 269

Chapter 29 · Snow Statuary 270

Chapter 30 · Sleds Chair-Sleighs and Snow-Shoes ... 274

A Chair-Sleigh 275
Folding Chair-Sleigh 276
The Toboggan 277
Snow-Shoes or Skates 278
Barrel-stave Show-shoe 280

Chapter 31 · The Winged Skaters and How to Make the Wings   282

➤ Bat Wings   284
➤ The Norton Rig   285
➤ The Norwegian Rig   287
➤ The Danish Rig   287
➤ The English Rig   288
➤ The Cape Vincent Rig   288
➤ A Country Rig   290

☞ PREFACE ☜

UNLESS boys have materially changed their habits in the last few years, it matters little what the preface of this book may contain, for it will be "skipped" without a passing glance. Still, in the established order of things, a preface, even if unnoticed by younger readers, is necessary to enable the author to state his purposes in undertaking the work, and to modestly put forward his claims on public attention.

It is the memory of the longing, that used to possess myself and my boy friends of a few years ago, for a real practical *American* boy's book, that has induced me to offer this volume.

The sports, amusements, and games embraced in this book are intended to reach the average American boy of any age, not too young to fly a kite or too old to enjoy a day's good fishing.

The book is based upon personal experiments and experiences, and is free, as far as lay within my power to make it, of foreign or technical terms or phrases.

Well do I remember the impracticable chemical experiments, necessitating professional skill and the use of complicated and expensive apparatus, the impossible feats of legerdemain and the time-worn conundrums, riddles, and games that help to make up the contents of the boy's books of my youth.

Unfamiliar and foreign terms, references to London shops as places to procure the articles mentioned, glittering generalities, and a general disregard for details are the marked characteristics of the books to which I refer.

Never shall I forget the disappointment experienced, when after consulting the index, I sought the article on paper balloons and found only the bare statement of the fact that balloons made of paper and filled with heated air *would ascend*. If I remember aright, the whole description occupies less than four lines.

Although the greater portion of the contents of the present volume has never been published before, some of it appeared as short articles in the *St. Nicholas Magazine;* and the directions and descriptions then given have been tested by thousands of boys throughout the United States, and, judging from the letters I have received, with uniform success.

Of course, such a book cannot, in the nature of things, be exhaustive, nor is it, indeed, desirable that it should be. Its use and principal purpose are to stimulate the inventive faculties in boys, to bring them face to face with practical emergencies when no book can supply the place of their own common sense and the exercise of personal intelligence and ingenuity.

Many new ideas will suggest themselves to the practical, ready-witted American boy, many simplifications and improvements on the apparatus here described; but it is hoped and expected by the author that the directions here given, as far as they go, will be found intelligible and practicable.

Nor is the volume, as is too often the case with this class of books, only to be made use of by lads with an almost unlimited supply of money at their disposal.

All apparatus described are either to be constructed of material easily obtained by almost any boy without cost, or by a very small outlay.

The author would also suggest to parents and guardians that money spent on fancy sporting apparatus, toys, etc., would be better spent upon tools and appliances.

Let boys *make their own kites and bows and arrows;* they will find a double pleasure in them, and value them accordingly, to say nothing of the education involved in the successful construction of their home-made playthings.

The development of a love of harmless fun is itself no valueless consideration. The baneful and destroying pleasures that offer themselves with an almost irresistible fascination to idle and unoccupied minds find no place with healthy activity and hearty interest in boyhood sports.

PART I
THE BOY CAMPER

CHAPTER 1

KNOTS BENDS & HITCHES

THE art of tying knots is an almost necessary adjunct to not a few recreations. Especially is this true of summer sports, many of which are nautical, or in some manner connected with the water.

Any boy who has been aboard a yacht or a sail-boat, must have realized that the safety of the vessel and all aboard may be imperilled by ignorance or negligence in the tying of a knot or fastening of a rope.

With some, the knack of tying a good, strong knot in a heavy rope, or light cord, seems to be a natural gift; it is certainly a very convenient accomplishment, and one that with practice and a little perseverance may be acquired even by those who at first make the most awkward and bungling attempts.

A bulky, cumbersome knot is not only ungainly, but is generally insecure.

As a rule, the strength of a knot is in direct proportion to its neat and handsome appearance.

To my mind, it is as necessary that the archer should know how to make the proper loops at the end of his bow-string, as it is that a hunter should understand how to load his gun.

Every fisherman should be able to join two lines neatly and securely, and should know the best and most expeditious method of attaching an extra hook or fly; and any boy who rigs up a hammock or swing with a "granny," or other insecure knot, deserves the ugly tumble and

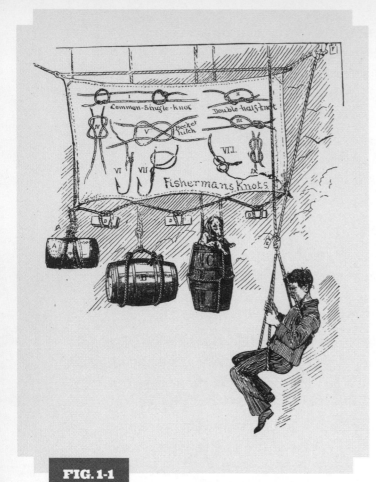

FIG. 1-1

sore bones that are more than liable to result from his ignorance.

A knot, nautically speaking, is a "bend" that is more permanent than a "hitch." A knot properly tied never slips, nor does it jam so that it cannot be readily untied. A "hitch" might be termed a temporary bend, as it is seldom relied upon for permanent service. The "hitch" is so made that it can be cast off, or unfastened, more quickly than a knot.

It is impossible for the brightest boy to learn to make "knots, bends, and hitches" by simply reading over a description of the methods; for, although he may understand them at the time, five minutes after reading the article the process will have escaped his memory; but if he take a piece of cord or rope, and sit down with the diagrams in front of him, he will find little difficulty in managing the most complicated knots; and he will not only acquire an accomplishment from which he can derive infinite amusement for himself and a means of entertainment for others, but the knowledge gained may, in case of accident by fire or flood, be the means of saving both life and property.

The accompanying diagrams show a number of useful and important bends, etc. To simplify matters, let us commence with **FIG. 1-1**, and go through the diagrams in the order in which they come:

The "English," or "common single fisherman's knot" (**FIG. 1-1**, I.), is neat and strong enough for any ordinary strain. The diagram shows the knots before being tightened and drawn together.

When exceptional strength is required it can be obtained by joining the lines in the ordinary single fisherman's knot (**FIG. 1-1**, I.), and pulling each of the half knots as tight as possible, then drawing them within an eighth of an inch of each other and wrapping between with fine gut that has been previously softened in water, or with light-colored silk.

An additional line, or a sinker may be attached by tying a knot in the end of the extra line, and inserting it between the parts of the single fisherman's knot before they are drawn together and tightened.

The "fisherman's double half knot," **FIG. 1-1** (II. and III.). After the gut has been passed around the main line and through itself, it is passed around the line once more and through the same loop again, and drawn close.

➻ **FIG. 1-1** (IV., V. and IX.). Here are three methods of joining the ends of two lines together; the diagrams explain them much better than words can. Take a piece of string, try each one, and test their relative strength.

➻ **FIG. 1-1** (VI.). It often happens, while fishing, that a hook is caught in a snag, or by some other means lost. The diagram shows the most expeditious manner of attaching another hook by what is known as the "sinker hitch," described further on (**FIG. 1-1**, D, and **FIG. 1-5**, XIV., XV., and XVI.).

➻ **FIG. 1-1**, VII. is another and more secure method of attaching a hook by knitting the line on with a succession of hitches.

How To Make a Horse-Hair Watch-Guard

The same hitches are used in the manufacture of horse-hair watch-guards, much in vogue with the boys in some sections of the country. As regularly as "kite-time," "top-time," or "ball-time," comes "horse-hair watch-guard time."

About once a year the rage for making watch-guards used to seize the boys of our school, and by some means or other almost every boy would have a supply of horse-hair on hand. With the first tap of the bell for recess, some fifty hands would dive into the mysterious depths of about fifty pockets, and before the bell had stopped ringing about fifty watch-guards, in a more or less incomplete state, would be produced.

Whenever a teamster's unlucky stars caused him to stop near the school-house, a chorus of voices greeted him with "Mister, please let us have some hair from your horses' tails."

The request was at first seldom refused, possibly because its nature was not at the time properly understood; but lucky was the boy considered who succeeded in pulling a supply of hair from the horses' tails without being interrupted by the heels of the animals or by the teamster, who, when he saw the swarm of boys tugging at his horses' tails, generally repented his first good-natured assent, and with a gruff "Get out, you young rascals!" sent the lads scampering to the school-yard fence.

Select a lot of long hair of the color desired; make it into a switch about the eighth of an inch thick by tying one end in a simple knot. Pick out a good, long hair and tie it around the switch close to the knotted end; then take the free end of the single hair in your right hand and pass it under the switch on one side, thus forming a loop through which the end of the hair must pass after it is brought up and over from the other side of the switch. Draw the knot tight by pulling the free end of the hair as shown by **FIG. 1-1**, VII. Every time this operation is repeated a wrap and a knot is produced. The knots follow each other in a spiral around the switch, giving it a very pretty, ornamented appearance. When one hair is used up select another, and commence knitting with it as you did with the first, being careful to cover and conceal the short end of the first hair, and to make the knots on the second commence where the former stop. A guard made of white horse-hair looks as if it might be composed of spun glass, and produces a very odd and pretty effect. A black one is very genteel in appearance.

Miscellaneous

➺ **FIG. 1-1**, VIII. shows a simple and expeditious manner of attaching a trolling hook to a fish-line.

➤ **FIG. 1-1**, F is a hitch used on shipboard, or wherever lines and cables are used. It is called the Blackwall hitch.

➤ **FIG. 1-1**, E is a fire-escape made of a double bowline knot, useful as a sling for hoisting persons up or letting them down from any high place; the window of a burning building, for instance. **FIG. 1-6**, XVIII., XIX. and XX. show how this knot is made. It is described on page 9.

➤ **FIG. 1-1**, A is a "bale hitch," made of a loop of rope. To make it, take a piece of rope that has its two ends joined; lay the rope down and place the bale on it; bring the loop opposite you up, on that side of the bale, and the loop in front up, on the side of the bale next to you; thrust the latter loop under and through the first and attach the hoisting rope. The heavier the object to be lifted, the tighter the hitch becomes. An excellent substitute for a shawl-strap can be made of a cord by using the bale hitch, the loop at the top being a first-rate handle.

➤ **FIG. 1-1**, B is called a cask sling, and C (**FIG. 1-1**) is called a butt sling. The manner of making these last two and their uses may be seen by referring to the illustration. It will be noticed that a line is attached to the bale hitch in a peculiar manner (A, **FIG. 1-1**). This is called the "anchor bend." If while aboard a sail-boat you have occasion to throw a bucket over for water, you will find the anchor bend a very convenient and safe way to attach a line to the bucket handle.

➤ **FIG. 1-2**, I. and II. are loops showing the elements of the simplest knots.

➤ **FIG. 1-2**, III. is a simple knot commenced.

➤ **FIG. 1-2**, IV. shows the simple knot tightened.

FIG. 1-2

FIG. 1-3

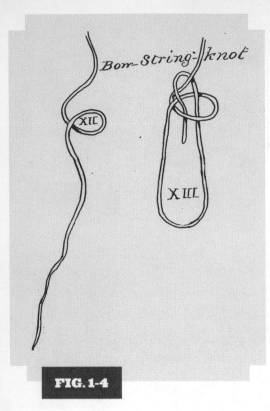

FIG. 1-4

⇒ **FIG. 1-2** V. and VI. show how the Flemish knot looks when commenced and finished.

⇒ **FIG. 1-3**, VII. and VIII. show a "rope knot" commenced and finished.

⇒ **FIG. 1-3**, IX. is a double knot commenced.

⇒ **FIG. 1-3**, X. is the same completed.

⇒ **FIG. 1-3**, XI. shows a back view of the double knot.

⇒ **FIG. 1-4**, XII. is the first loop of a "bowline knot." One end of the line is supposed to be made fast to some object. After the turn or loop (**FIG. 1-4**, XII.) is made, hold it in position with your left hand and pass the end of the line up through the loop or turn you have just made, behind and over the line above, then down through the loop again, as shown in the diagram (**FIG. 1-4**, XIII.); pull it tight and the knot is complete. The "sinker hitch" is a very handy one to know, and the variety of uses it may be put to will be at once suggested by the diagrams.

Lines that have both ends made fast may have weights attached to them by means of the sinker hitch (**FIG. 1-1**, D).

To accomplish this, first gather up some slack and make it in the form of the loop (**FIG. 1-5**, XIV); bend the loop back on itself (Fig. **1-5**, XV.) and slip the weight through the double loop thus formed (**FIG. 1-5**, XVI.); draw tight by pulling the two top lines, and the sinker hitch is finished (**FIG. 1-5**, XVII.).

The "fire-escape sling" previously mentioned, and illustrated by **FIG. 1-1**, E, is made with a double line.

FIG. 1-5

Proceed at first as you would to make a simple bowline knot (**FIG. 1-6**, XVIII.).

After you have run the end loop up through the turn (**FIG. 1-6**, XIX.), bend it downward and over the bottom loop and turn, then up again until it is in the position shown in **FIG. 1-6**, XX.; pull it downward until the knot is tightened, as in **FIG. 1-1**, E, and it makes a safe sling in which to lower a person from any height. The longer loop serves for a seat, and the shorter one, coming under the arms, makes a rest for the back.

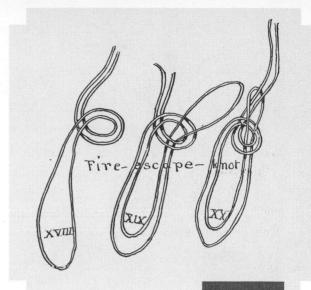

FIG. 1-6

»→ **FIG. 1-7**, XXI. is called a "boat knot," and is made with the aid of a stick. It is an excellent knot for holding weights which may want instant detachment. To detach it, lift the weight slightly and push out the stick, and instantly the knot is untied.

»→ **FIG. 1-7**, XXII. Commencement of a "six-fold knot."

»→ **FIG. 1-7**, XXIII. Six-fold knot completed by drawing the two ends with equal force. A knot drawn in this manner is said to be "nipped."

»→ **FIG. 1-8**, XXIV. A simple hitch or "double" used in making loop knots.

»→ **FIG. 1-8**, XXV. "Loop knot."

»→ **FIG. 1-8**, XXVI. shows how the loop knot is commenced.

»→ **FIG. 1-8**, XXVII. is the "Dutch double knot," sometimes called the "Flemish loop."

»→ **FIG. 1-8**, XXVIII. shows a common "running knot."

»→ **FIG. 1-8**, XXIX. A running knot with a check knot to hold.

FIG. 1-7

»→ **FIG. 1-8**, XXX. A running knot checked.

»→ **FIG. 1-8**, XXXI. The right hand part of the rope shows how to make the double loop for the "twist knot." The left hand part of the same rope shows a finished twist knot. It is made by taking a half turn on both the

FIG. 1-8

right hand and left hand lines of the double loop, and passing the end through the "bight" (loop) so made.

Whip-Lashes

➻ **FIG. 1-9**, XXXII. is called the "chain knot," which is often used in braiding leather whip-lashes. To make a "chain knot," fasten one end of the thong or line; make a simple loop and pass it over the left hand; retain hold of the free end with the right hand; with the left hand seize the line above the right hand and draw a loop through the loop already formed; finish the knot by drawing it tight with the left hand. Repeat the operation until the braid is of the required length, then secure it by passing the free end through the last loop.

➻ **FIG. 1-9**, XXXIII. shows a double chain knot.

➻ **FIG. 1-9**, XXXIV. is a double chain knot pulled out. It shows how the free end is thrust through the last loop.

➻ **FIG. 1-9**, XXXV. Knotted loop for end of rope, used to prevent the end of the rope from slipping, and for various other purposes.

Timber-Hitches, etc.

➻ **FIG. 1-10**, A. Combination of half hitch and timber hitch.

➻ **FIG. 1-10**, B. Ordinary half hitch.

➻ **FIG. 1-10**, C. Ordinary timber hitch.

➻ **FIG. 1-10**, D. Another timber hitch, called the "clove hitch."

➻ **FIG. 1-10**, E. "Hammock hitch," used for binding bales of goods or cloth.

➻ **FIG. 1-11**, F. "Lark-head knot," used by sailors and boatmen for mooring their crafts.

➻ **FIG. 1-11**, P shows a lark-head fastening to a running knot.

➻ **FIG. 1-11**, G is a double-looped lark-head.

➻ **FIG. 1-11**, H shows a double-looped lark-head knot fastened to the ring of a boat.

FIG. 1-9

➵ **FIG. 1-11**, I is a "treble lark-head." To make it you must first tie a single lark-head, then divide the two heads and use each singly, as shown in the diagram.

FIG. 1-10

➵ **FIG. 1-11**, J shows a simple boat knot with one turn.

➵ **FIG. 1-11**, K. "Crossed running knot." It is a strong and handy tie, not as difficult to make as appears to be.

FIG. 1-11

➵ **FIG. 1-11**, L is the bowline knot, described by the diagrams XII. and XIII. (**FIG. 1-4**). The free end of the knot is made fast by binding it to the "bight" or the loop. It makes a secure sling for a man to sit in at his work among the rigging.

➵ **FIG. 1-11**, M, N, and O. "Slip clinches," or "sailors' knots."

➵ **FIG. 1-12**, Q shows a rope fastened by the chain hitch. The knot at the left-hand end explains a simple way to prevent a rope from unravelling.

➵ **FIG. 1-13**, R. A timber hitch; when tightened the line binds around the timber so that it will not slip.

➵ **FIG. 1-13**, S. Commencement of simple lashing knot.

➵ **FIG. 1-13**, T. Simple lashing knot finished.

➵ **FIG. 1-13**, U. "Infallible loop;" not properly a timber hitch, but useful in a variety of ways, and well adapted for use in archery.

FIG. 1-12

FIG. 1-13

➣ **FIG. 1-13**, V. Same as R, reversed. It looks like it might give way under a heavy strain, but it will not.

➣ **FIG. 1-13**, W. Running knot with two ends.

➣ **FIG. 1-13**, X. Running knot with a check knot that can only be opened with a marline-spike.

➣ **FIG. 1-13**, Y. A two-ended running knot with a check to the running loops. This knot can be untied by drawing both ends of the cord.

➣ **FIG. 1-13**, Z. Running knot with two ends, fixed by a double Flemish knot. When you wish to encircle a timber with this tie, pass the ends, on which the check knot is to be, through the cords before they are drawn tight. This will require considerable practice.

➣ **FIG. 1-13**, *a* shows an ordinary twist knot.

➣ **FIG. 1-13**, *a'* shows the form of loop for builder's knot.

➣ **FIG. 1-13**, *b*. Double twist knot.

➣ **FIG. 1-13**, *c*. Builder's knot finished.

➣ **FIG. 1-13**, *d* represents a double builder's knot.

➣ **FIG. 1-14**, *e*. "Weaver's knot," same as described under the head of Becket hitch (**FIG. 1-2**, V).

➣ **FIG. 1-14**, *f*. Weaver's knot drawn tight.

➣ **FIG. 1-14**, *g* shows how to commence a reef knot. This is useful for small ropes; with ropes unequal in size the knot is likely to draw out of shape, as *m*.

➣ **FIG. 1-14**, *h* shows a reef knot completed.

➣ Of all knots, avoid the "granny;" it is next to useless under a strain, and marks the tier as a "landlubber."

➣ **FIG. 1-14**, *i* shows a granny knot; *n* shows a granny under strain.

FIG. 1-14

⇒ **FIG. 1-14**, *j* shows the commencement of a common "rough knot."

⇒ **FIG. 1-14**, *k*. The front view of finished knot.

⇒ **FIG. 1-14**, *l*. The back view of finished knot. Although this knot will not untie nor slip, the rope is likely to part at one side if the strain is great. Awkward as it looks, this tie is very useful at times on account of the rapidity with which it can be made.

⇒ **FIG. 1-14**, *o* and *p*. Knot commenced and finished, used for the same purposes as the Flemish knot.

⇒ **FIG. 1-14**, *q* and *q'*. An ordinary knot with the ends used separately.

⇒ **FIG. 1-15**, *s*. Sheep-shank, or dog-shank as it is sometimes called, is very useful in shortening a line. Suppose, for instance, a swing is much longer than necessary, and you wish to shorten it without climbing aloft to do so; it can be done with a sheep-shank.

⇒ **FIG. 1-15**, *r* shows the first position of the two loops. Take two half hitches, and you have a bend of the form shown by *s*. Pull tightly from above and below the shank, and you will find that the rope is shortened securely enough for ordinary strain.

⇒ **FIG. 1-15**, *t*. Shortening by loop and turns made where the end of the rope is free.

⇒ **FIG. 1-15**, *u*. A shortened knot that can be used when either end is free.

⇒ **FIG. 1-15**, *v*, *w*, and *x*. Shortening knots.

⇒ **FIG. 1-16**, *y* and *z*. A "true lover's knot," and the last one that you need to practise on, for one of these knots is as much as most persons can attend to, and ought to last a lifetime.

FIG. 1-15

FIG. 1-16

CHAPTER 2

HOW
TO CAMP OUT
WITHOUT
A TENT

THE next best thing to really living in the woods is talking over such an experience. A thousand little incidents, scarcely thought of at the time, crowd upon my mind, and bring back with them the feeling of freedom and adventure so dear to the heart of every boy. Shall I ever enjoy any flavor earth can afford as we did our coffee a-field? The flapjacks—how good and appetizing! the fish—how delicate and sweet! And the wonderful cottage of boughs, thatched with the tassels of the pine—was there ever a cottage out of a fairy tale that could compare with it?

In fancy I can see it now. There stands the little cot, flooded with the light of the setting sun; those who built it and use it for a habitation are off exploring, hunting, fishing, and foraging for their evening meal, and the small, shy creatures of the wood take the opportunity to satisfy the curiosity with which they have, from a safe distance, viewed the erection of so large and singular a nest.

The boys will soon return, each with his contribution to the larder—a fish, a squirrel, a bird, or a rabbit, which will be cooked and eaten with better appetite and enjoyment than the most elaborate viands that home could afford. And although such joys are denied to me now, I can, at least, in remembering them, give others an opportunity to possess similar pleasures. It shall be my object to describe how these houses may be built and these dinners cooked, and that, too, where there are neither planks, nor nails, nor stoves. To boys well informed in woodcraft, only a few hints need be given; but for the benefit of amateurs we will go more into detail.

The Rustic Cottage

Four persons make a good camping-party. Before arriving at their destination these persons should choose one of their number as captain.

The captain gives directions and superintends the pitching of the tent or the building of the rustic cottage. The site for the camp should be upon a knoll, mound, or rising ground, so as to afford a good drainage. If the forest abounds in pine trees, the young cottage-builder's task is an easy one. It often happens that two or three trees already standing

FIG. 2-1

Frame of the Cottage

can be made to serve for the corners of the proposed edifice, though trees for corners are not absolutely necessary.

FIG. 2-1 represents part of the framework of one of the simplest forms of rustic cottage. In this case, two trees serve for the two posts of the rear wall. The front posts are young trees that have been cut down and firmly planted at about four or five paces in front of the trees, as shown in the illustration. Enough

FIG. 2-2

The way to Thatch

of the branches have been left adhering to the trunks of the upright posts to serve as rests for the cross bars. To prevent complication in the diagram, the roof is not shown. To make this, fasten on an additional cross bar or two to the rear wall, then put a pole at each side, slanting down from the rear to the front, and cover these poles with cross sticks. When the framework is finished, the security and durability of the structure will be improved by fastening all the loose joints, tying them together with withes of willow, grass, or reeds. The next step is to cover the frame. This is done after the method shown in **FIG. 2-2**. From among some boughs, saved for this purpose, take one and hang it upon the third cross bar, counting from the ground up; bring the bough down, passing it inside the second bar and resting the end on the ground outside the first bar; repeat this with other boughs until the row is finished. Then begin at the fourth bar, passing the boughs down inside the third and outside the second bar, so that they will overlap the first row. Continue in this manner until the four walls are closed in, leaving spaces open where windows or doors are wanted. The roof is thatched after the same method, beginning at the front and working upward and backward to the rear wall, each row overlapping the preceding row of thatch. The more closely and compactly you thatch the roof and walls, the better protection will they afford from any passing shower. This completed, the house is finished, and you will be astonished to see what a lovely little green cot you have built.

A cottage may be built differing from the one we have just described by having the roof extended so as to form a sort of verandah, or porch, in front; the floor of the porch may be covered with a layer of pine-needles. Should you find your house too small to accommodate your party, you can, by erecting a duplicate cottage four or five paces at one side, and roofing over the intervening space, have a house of two rooms with an open hall-way between.

The Bedstead

Before going to housekeeping, some furniture will be necessary; and for this we propose to do our shopping right in the neighborhood of our cottage. Here is our cabinet and upholstery shop, in the wholesome fragrance of the pines.

After the labor of building, your thoughts will naturally turn to a place for sleeping. Cut four forked sticks, sharpen the ends, and drive them firmly into the ground at the spot where you wish the bed to stand in your room. Two strong poles, long enough to reach lengthwise from fork to fork, will serve for side boards; a number of short sticks will answer for slats; after these are fastened in place you have the rustic bedstead shown in **FIG. 2-3**. A good spring mattress is very desirable, and not difficult to obtain. Gather a lot of small green branches, or brush, and cover your bedstead with a layer of it about one foot thick; this you will find a capital substitute for springs. For your mattress proper, go to your upholstery shop under the pine tree and gather several armfuls of the dry pine-needles; cover the elastic brush *springs* with a thick layer of these needles; over this spread your India-rubber

FIG. 2-3

Bedstead

blanket, with the rubber side under, so that any moisture or dampness there may be in your mattress may be prevented from coming through. You may now make up your bed with what wraps or blankets you have with you, and you have (**FIG. 2-4**) as complete and comfortable a bed as any forester need wish for. In the place of pine-needles, hay or grass may be used. I have slept very comfortably upon a brush mattress covered with iron-weed.*

FIG. 2-4

Bed made up

I would suggest to any boy who means to try this rustic cabinet-making, to select carefully for the bed-posts sticks strong enough to support the weight he intends them to bear, otherwise his slumbers may be interrupted in an abrupt and disagreeable manner. My first experiment in this line proved disastrous. I spent the greater part of one day in building and neatly finishing a bed like the one described. After it was made up, with an army blanket for a coverlid, it looked so soft, comfortable, and inviting that I scarcely could wait for bed-time to try it.

When the evening meal was over and the last story told around the blazing camp-fire, I took off hat, coat, and boots and snuggled down in my new and original couch, curiously watched by my companions, who lay, rolled in their blankets, upon the hard ground. It does not take a boy long to fall asleep, particularly after a hard day's work in the open air, but it takes longer, after being aroused from a sound nap, for him to get his wits together—especially when suddenly dumped upon the ground with a crash, amid a heap of broken sticks and dry brush, as I happened to be on that eventful night. Loud and long were the shouts of laughter of my companions when they discovered my misfortune. Theoretically, the bed was well planned, but practically it was a failure, because it had rotten sticks for bed-posts.

---

* Iron-weed; flat-top (Vernonia noveboracensis); a common Kentucky weed, with beautiful purple blossoms.

FIG. 2-5

Barrel in Bank

Old Barrel Oven

Having provided bed and shelter, it is high time to look after the inner boy; and while the foragers are off in search of provisions, it will be the cook's duty to provide some method of cooking the food that will be brought in.

One of the simplest and most practical forms of bake-oven can be made of clay and an old barrel. Remove one head of the barrel, scoop out a space in the nearest bank, and fit the barrel in (**FIG. 2-5**). If the mud or clay is not damp enough, moisten it and plaster it over the barrel to the depth of a foot or more, leaving a place for a chimney at the back end, where part of a stave has been cut away; around this place build a chimney of sticks arranged log-cabin fashion and plastered with mud (**FIG. 2-6**). After this, make a good, rousing fire in the barrel, and keep adding fuel until all the staves are burned out and the surrounding clay is baked hard. This makes an oven that will bake as well, if not better, than any new patented stove or range at home. To use it, build a fire inside and let it burn until the oven

FIG. 2-6

Heating the Oven

is thoroughly heated, then rake out all the coal and embers, put your dinner in and close up the front with the head of the barrel preserved for this purpose. The clay will remain, hot for several hours and keep the inside of the oven hot enough to roast meat or bake bread.

Stone Stove

If there be no bank convenient, or if you have no barrel with which to build this style of oven, there are other methods that will answer for all the cooking necessary to a party of boys camping out. Many rare fish have I eaten in my time. The delicious pompano at New Orleans, the brook-trout and grayling, fresh from the cold water of Northern Michigan, but never have I had fish taste better than did a certain large cat-fish that we boys once caught on a set-line in Kentucky. We built a fire-place of flat stones, a picture of which you have in **FIG. 2-7**, covered it with a thin piece of slate, cleaned the fish and with its skin still on, placed it upon the slate. When it was brown upon one side we turned it over until it was thoroughly cooked. With green sticks we lifted off the fish and placed it upon a piece of clean bark; the skin adhered to the stone, and the meat came off in the smoking, snowy pieces, which we ate with the aid of our pocket-knives and rustic forks made of small green twigs with the forked ends sharpened.

If stones cannot be had to answer for this stove, there still remains old, primitive camp-fire and pot-hook. The very sight of this iron pot

FIG. 2-7

A Stone Stove

FIG. 2-8

A Butter-Knife

swinging over a blazing fire suggests soup, to eat which with any comfort spoons are necessary. These are quickly and easily made by thrusting clam or mussel shells into splits made in the ends of sticks. A splendid butter-knife can be made from the shell of a razor-oyster with a little care in a similar manner (see **FIG. 2-8**).

Rustic Chair and Camp Table

If you stay any time in your forest home you can, by a little ingenuity, add many comforts and conveniences. I have drawn some diagrams, as hints, in this direction. For instance, **FIG. 2-9** shows the manner of making an excellent rustic chair of two stout poles and two cross poles, to which are fastened the ends of a piece of canvas, carpet or leather (**FIG. 2-10**), which, swinging loose, fits itself exactly to your form, making a most comfortable easy-chair in which to rest or take a nap after a hard day's tramp. It often happens that the peculiar formation of some stump or branch suggests new styles of seats. A table can

FIG. 2-9

Frame of Rustic Chair

be very readily made by driving four forked sticks into the ground for legs, and covering the cross sticks upon the top with pieces of birch or other smooth bark. **FIG. 2-11** shows a table made in this manner, with one piece of bark removed to reveal its construction.

As a general rule, what is taught in boys' books, though correct in theory, when tried proves impracticable. This brings to mind an incident that happened to a party of young hunters camping out in Ohio. Early one morning one of the boys procured from a distant farmhouse a dozen pretty little white bantam eggs. Having no game, and only one small fish in the way of fresh meat, the party congratulated themselves upon the elegant breakfast they would make of fresh eggs, toasted crackers, and coffee. How to cook the eggs was the question. One of the party proposed his plan.

"I have just read a book," said he, "which tells how some travellers cooked fowls and fish by rolling them up in clay and tossing them into the fire. Shall we try that plan with the eggs?"

The rest of the party assented, and soon all were busy rolling rather large balls of blue clay, in the centre of each of which was an egg. A dozen were placed in the midst of the hottest embers, and the boys seated themselves around the fire, impatiently waiting for the eggs to cook. They did cook—with a vengeance! Zip, bang! went one, then another and another, until, in less time than it takes to tell it, not an egg remained unexploded; and the hot embers and bits of clay that stuck to the boys' hair and clothes were all that was left to remind them of those nice, fresh bantam eggs. It was all very funny, but ever after the boys of that party showed the greatest caution in trying new schemes, no matter how well they might seem to be endorsed.

FIG. 2-10

The Rustic Chair Finished

Hints to Amateur Campers

From time immemorial it has been the custom of the city fellows to laugh at their country cousins, and to poke all manner of fun at them on account of their verdancy in regard to city manners and customs. This is hardly fair, for if a real city fellow be placed on a farm, or in the woods, his ignorance is just as laughable and absurd. It was only the other day I saw a young New York artist refuse to drink from a spring because something *was bubbling up at the bottom.* Experience is a great teacher. Even the artist just mentioned, after making himself sick

FIG. 2-11

A Camp Table

upon stagnant water, would, no doubt, learn to select bubbling springs in the future. A few timely hints may, however, prevent many mishaps and unpleasant accidents.

Provisions

It is always desirable to take as large a stock of provisions as can be conveniently transported. In these, days of canned meats, soups, vegetables, and fruits, a large amount of provisions may be stored in a small space. Do not fail to take a plentiful supply of salt, pepper, and sugar; also bacon, flour, meal, grits, or hominy, tea, coffee, and condensed milk. If you have any sort of luck with your rod, gun, or traps, the forest and stream ought to supply fresh meat, and with the appetite only enjoyed by people who live out doors you can "live like a king."

Shelter

Because I have described but one sort of shelter my readers must not suppose that it is absolutely necessary to build a cottage like the one described. On the contrary, there are a thousand different plans that will suggest themselves to fellows who are accustomed to camping out. The huts, or sheds, built of "slabs" by some of the Adirondack hunters are very convenient, but unless the open ends are protected, in time of a storm, the rain is apt to drive in and soak the inmates. The two sheds face each other, and in the middle of the space between the camp-fire blazes, throwing a ruddy light at night into both compartments.

By taking advantage of a rock, a fallen or uprooted tree, the work of building a hut is ofttimes materially lessened.

Tents, of course, are very handy and comfortable, and if obtainable should by all means be used. At least one or two good sharp hatchets should form a part of the equipment of every camp; it is astonishing, with their aid and a little practice, what a comfortable house may be built in a very short time.

Choosing Companions

Never join a camping party that has among its members a single peevish, irritable, or selfish person, or a "shirk." Although the company of such a boy may be only slightly annoying at school or upon the play-ground, in camp the companionship of a fellow of this description becomes unbearable. Even if the game fill the woods and the waters are alive with fish, an irritable or selfish companion will spoil all the fun and take the sunshine out of the brightest day. The whole party should be composed of fellows who are willing to take things as they come and make the best of everything. With such companions there is no such thing as "bad luck;" rain or shine everything is always jolly, and when you return from the woods, strengthened in mind and body, you will always remember with pleasure your camping experience.

CHAPTER 3

SNOW HOUSES

IN "the land of the midnight sun," the far arctic regions where Jack Frost rules supreme, where the glistening ice and thickly packed snow covers the landscape almost the whole year round, the hardy inhabitants live in huts built of frozen blocks of snow. The interior of these icy dwellings are not, as might be supposed, uncomfortably cold, but, on the contrary, are quite warm and cosey. Boys who are inclined to doubt this may make the experiment for themselves. After the first good old-fashioned snow storm has covered the play-ground, roads, and house-tops, and while the merry jingle of the sleigh-bells tinkles through the wintry air let them busy themselves rolling huge balls of snow after the manner described in the chapter on "Snowball Warfare," making the foundation of the house exactly in the same way as that described for the snow-fort.

The roof is made of boards or planks covered with snow. A barrel placed over a hole in the roof, and surrounded by packed snow properly shaped, will make a very good chimney. A pane of glass can be set

FIG. 3-1

A Snow-House under contruction

FIG. 3-2

*A Snow-House
finished*

in the square hole made for a window; a heavy piece of carpet can be hung from the ceiling over the doorway, so as to act as a curtain; or if the young work-people choose to take trouble enough, they can put up a framework inside of the door-way and hang a wooden door to it by leather or canvas hinges. An old stove, or a fire-place made near the wall under the chimney, adds a finish to the house that will be found quite snug and comfortable as long as the snow lasts. The fire inside, if the weather be cold, will not melt the walls. The pictures of the house (**FIGS. 3-1** and **3-2**) show so well how it is constructed, and how it looks when it is done, that very little explanation is necessary.

The walls are made of large snow-balls properly placed, with snow packed between them to make the surfaces tolerably even, and then the whole shaved down with a spade, outside and inside. It will be found impossible to put one tier of balls upon the top of the others by lifting them in place, but this difficulty may be overcome by sliding the balls up an inclined plane made of a strong plank, one end of which must be placed upon the ground and the other allowed to rest upon the top of the first or foundation row of snowballs.

PART II

THE BOY BOATER

CHAPTER 4

HOME-MADE BOATS

Birth of the "Man-Friday" Catamaran

Not so very many years ago I remember visiting, in company with my cousin Tom, a small lake at the head waters of the Miami. High and precipitous cliffs surround the little body of water. So steep were the great weather-beaten rocks that it was only where the stream came tumbling down past an old mill that an accessible path then existed. Down that path Tom and I scrambled, for we knew that large bass lurked in the deep, black holes among the rocks.

We had no jointed split bamboo rods nor fancy tackle, but the fish there in those days were not particular and seldom hesitated to bite at an angle-worm or grasshopper, though the hook upon which the bait squirmed was suspended by a coarse line from a freshly cut hickory sapling.

Even now I feel the thrill of excitement and expectancy as, in imagination, my pole is bent nearly double by the frantic struggles of those "gamy" black bass. After spending the morning fishing we built a fire upon a short stretch of sandy beach, and cleaning our fish and washing them in the spring close at hand, we put them among the embers to cook.

While the fire was getting our dinner ready for us we threw off our clothes and plunged into the cool waters of the lake. Inexpert swimmers as we were at that time, the opposite shore, though apparently

FIG. 4-1

The Man Friday

only a stone's-throw distant, was too far off for us to reach by swimming. Many a longing and curious glance we cast toward it, however, and strong was the temptation that beset us to try the unknown depths intervening. A pair of brown ears appeared above the ferns near the water's edge, and a fox peeped at us; squirrels ran about the fallen trunks of trees or scampered up the rocks as saucily as though they understood that we could not swim well enough to reach their side of the lake; and high up the face of the cliff was a dark spot which we almost knew to be the entrance to some mysterious cavern.

How we longed for a boat! But not even a raft nor a dugout could be seen anywhere upon the glassy surface of the water or along its reedy border. We nevertheless determined to explore the lake next day, even if we should have to paddle astride of a log.

The first rays of the morning sun had not reached the dark waters before my companion and I were hard at work, with axe and hatchet, chopping in twain a long log we had discovered near the mill. We had at first intended to build a raft; but gradually we evolved a sort of catamaran. The two pieces of log we sharpened at the ends for the bow; then we rolled the logs down upon the beach, and, while I went into the thicket to chop down some saplings, my companion borrowed an auger from the miller. We next placed the logs about three feet apart, and marking the points where we intended to put the cross-pieces, we cut notches there; then we placed the saplings across, fitting them into these notches. To hold them securely we bored holes down through the sapling cross-pieces into the logs; with the hatchet we hammered wooden pegs into these holes. For the seat we used the half of a section of log, the flat side fitting into places cut for that purpose. All that remained to be done now was to make a seat in the stern and a pair of rowlocks. At a proper distance from the oarsman's seat we bored two holes for a couple of forked sticks, which answered admirably for rowlocks; across the stern we fastened another piece of log, similar to that used for the oarsman's seat. With the help of a man from the mill our craft was launched; and with a pair of oars made of old pine boards we rowed off, leaving the miller waving his hat.

Our catamaran was not so light as a row-boat, but it floated, and we could propel it with the oars, and, best of all, it was our own invention and made with our own hands. We called it a "Man-Friday," and by its means we explored every nook in the length and breadth of the lake; and ever afterward when we wanted a boat we knew a simple and inexpensive way to make one—and a safe one, too.

The Crusoe Raft

is another rustic craft, but it is of more ambitious dimensions than the "Man-Friday." Instead of being able to float only one or two passengers, the "Crusoe," if properly built, ought to accommodate a considerable party of raftsmen. Of course the purpose for which the raft is to be used, and the number of the crew that is expected to man it, must be taken into consideration when deciding upon the dimensions of the proposed craft.

All the tools that are necessary for the construction of a good stout raft are an axe, an auger, and a hatchet, with some strong boys to wield them.

The building material can be gathered upon any wooded bank of lake or stream.

For a moderate sized raft collect six or seven logs, the longest not being over sixteen feet in length, nor more than a foot in diameter; the logs

FIG. 4-2

Plan of Crusoe raft

FIG. 4-3

Skeleton of Crusoe Raft

must be tolerably straight. Pick out the longest and biggest for the centre; sharpen one end; roll the log into the water and there secure it.

Select two logs as nearly alike as possible, to lie one at each side of the centre log. Measure the centre log, and make the point of each side log, not at its own centre, but at that side of it which will lie against the middle log, so that this side-point shall terminate where the pointing of the middle log begins. (See **FIG. 4-2**.)

After all the logs needed have been trimmed and sharpened in the manner just described, roll them into the water and arrange them in order (**FIG. 4-2**). Fasten them together with "cross-strips," boring holes through the strips to correspond with holes bored into the logs lying beneath, and through these holes drive wooden pegs. The water will cause the pegs to swell, and they will hold much more firmly than iron nails.

The skeleton of the cabin can be made of saplings; such as are used for hoop-poles are the best.

These are each bent into an arch, and the ends are thrust into holes bored for that purpose. Over this hooping a piece

FIG. 4-4

Crusoe with Cabin Covered

of canvas is stretched, after the manner of old-fashioned country wagons (**FIGS. 4-3** and **4-4**).

FIG. 4-5

Sweeps

Erect a "jack-staff," to be used as a flag-pole or a mast to rig a square sail on.

A stout stick should be erected at the stern, and a similar one upon each side of the raft near the bow; these sticks, when their ends are made smaller, as shown in the illustration (**FIG. 4-3**), serve as rowlocks.

For oars use "sweeps"—long poles, each with a piece of board for a blade fastened at one end (**FIG. 4-5**).

Holes must be bored through the poles of the sweeps about three feet from the handle, to slip over the pegs used as rowlocks, as described above. These pegs should be high enough to allow the oarsman to stand while using the sweeps.

A flat stone placed at the bow will serve as a fireplace.

If the cracks between the logs under the cabin are filled up to prevent the water splashing through, and the cabin is floored with cross-sticks, a most comfortable bed at night can be made of hay by heaping it under the canvas cover in sufficient quantities.

The "Crusoe" raft has this great advantage over all boats: you may take a long trip down the river, allowing the current to bear you along, using the sweeps only to assist the man at the helm (rear sweep); then, after your excursion is finished, you can abandon the raft and return by steamboat or cars.

Slab Canoe

The "Crusoe-raft" is an immense success, and the "Man Friday" has been used, not only by the boy readers of this book, but by the parents and big brothers of the boys in their hunting trips, and these rustic crafts may now be seen on many of the unfrequented lakes deep in

FIG. 4-6

the North Woods; in fact, these two simple and primitive boats have become so popular that the writer will add another to the list, if anything, still more primitive in design.

The advance-guard of modern civilization is the lumberman, and following close on his heels comes the all-devouring saw-mill. This fierce creature has an abnormal appetite for logs, and it keeps an army of men, boys, and horses busy in supplying it with food. And, while it supplies us with lumber for the carpenter, builder, and cabinet-maker, it at the same time, in the most shameful way, fills the trout-streams and rivers with great masses of sawdust, which kills and drives away the fish. But near the saw-mill there is always to be found material for a

The Slab Canoe, which consists simply of one of those long slabs, the first cut from some giant log. (**FIG. 4-6**.)

FIG. 4-7

These slabs are burned or thrown away by the mill-owners, and hence cost nothing; and as the saw-mill is in advance of population, you are most likely to run across one on a hunting or fishing trip.

Near one end, and on the flat side of the slab (**FIG. 4-6**), bore four holes, into which drive the four legs of a stool made of a section of a smaller slab (**FIG. 4-7**), and your boat is ready to launch. From a piece of board, make a double or single paddle (**FIG. 4-8**),

and you are equipped for a voyage. An old gentleman, who in his boyhood days on the frontier frequently used this simple style of canoe, says that the speed it makes will compare favorably with that of many a more pretentious vessel. See **FIG. 4-9** for furnished boat.

How to Build a Birch Bark Canoe

According to the Baltimore Sun, birch canoes are greatly increasing in popularity. At most of the summer reports they will soon supersede all other craft that have to be propelled by hand. There are several reasons for this renewal of favor. They are not hard to propel, they are pretty, and in experienced hands perfectly safe. They are also indispensable to sportsmen. So general is the favor in which these light and graceful boats are held that the building of them has become quite an industry in Maine, especially along the Penobscot River.

FIG. 4-8

Although the Indian was the first to build these simple little boats, some of his white brothers are quite as expert in the work. But the red man can outdo his white brother in navigating the craft. The only tools required in building a canoe are a knife and awl, a draw-shave and a hammer. An Indian can do all of his work with a knife.

Several years ago canvas began to be used extensively in canoe-building, instead of birch bark, but it will never entirely supersede birch, for nothing can be found that bends so gracefully. There are several canvas canoe factories in Maine, but the canoes made of canvas have neither the symmetry nor the durability of the birches. They are a trifle cheaper, however, but if pleasure and profit are wanted, one should never have anything but a bark craft.

FIG. 4-9

If properly handled, a good canoe will safely hold four men. Canoes intended for deep water should have considerable depth. Those intended for shoal water, such as trout fishers use, are made as flat as possible. Up to the time when canoeing was introduced the materials for building craft of this kind could be found all along the rivers. Big birch-trees grew in countless numbers, and clear, straight cedar was quite as plentiful within a few feet of the water's edge. Now one must go miles back into the dense forest for such materials, and even then seldom does it happen that two suitable trees are found within sight one of the other. Cedar is the harder of the two to find.

When the writer's young friend Mr. E. T. Adney, the artist, naturalist, and backwoodsman, returned from the North Woods, he told

Showing how the butt is kept off the ground

FIG. 4-10

the author that among other accomplishments he had learned how to build a real Indian birch bark canoe. His description of the manner in which this graceful boat is made was so interesting that the main points are here inserted for the benefit of those who are ambitious of becoming skilled in wood craft.

Indian Birch Bark Canoe

The Tree

The tree is selected, first, for straightness, second, smoothness, third, freedom from knots or limbs, fourth, toughness of bark, fifth small size of eyes, sixth, length—which last is not so important, as two trees can be put together—and seventh, size, which is also not so important, as the sides can be pieced out.

Torch

FIG. 4-11

Dimensions

The average length of canoe is about 19 feet over all, running, generally, from 18 to 22 feet for a boat to be used on inland waters, the sea-going canoes being larger, with relatively higher bows. The average width is about 30 inches inside, measured along the middle cross-bar; the greatest width inside is several inches below the middle cross-bar, and it is several inches greater than the width measured along said cross-bar.

The measurements given below are those of a canoe 19 feet over all; 16 feet long inside, measured along the curve of the gunwale; 30 inches wide inside. The actual length inside is less than 16 feet, but the measurement along the gunwales is the most important.

Bark

Bark can be peeled when the sap is flowing or when the tree is not frozen—at any time in late spring, summer, and early fall (called summer bark); in winter during a thaw, when the tree is not frozen, and when the sap may have begun to flow.

Difference in the Bark

Summer bark peels readily, is smooth inside, of a yellow color, which turns reddish upon exposure to the sun, and is chalky-gray in very old canoes. Winter bark adheres closely, and forcibly brings up part of the inner bark, which on exposure turns dark red. This rough surface may be moistened and scraped away. All winter-bark canoes must be thus scraped and made smooth. Sometimes the dark red is left in the form of a decorative pattern extending around the upper edge of the canoe, the rest of the surface being scraped smooth.

FIG. 4-12

Process of Peeling

The tree must be cut down so that the bark can be removed more easily.

A long, narrow notch (FIG. 4-11) is cut in the ground, a few feet from the base of the tree, which will keep the butt of the tree off the ground when the tree is felled. The limbs at the top will keep the other end off the ground. A space is cleared of bushes and obstructions where the tree is to fall.

After the tree has been cut down, a cut is made in a straight line (A, B, **FIG. 4-10**), splitting the bark from top to bottom, and a ring cut at A and B (**FIG. 4-10**). When sap is flowing, the bark is readily removed; but in winter, the edges of the cut are raised with a knife, and a thin, pliant hardwood knife or "spud" is pushed around the bark.

FIG. 4-13

Toasting

After the bark has dropped upon the ground, the inside surface is warmed with a torch, which

FIG. 4-14

FIG. 4-15

FIG. 4-16

softens and straightens it out flat. The torch is made of a bundle of birch bark held in a splitstick (**FIG. 4-11**).

It is then rolled up like a carpet, with inside surface out, and tightly bound, generally with cedar bark when the latter can be procured (**FIG. 4-12**).

If the tree is long enough, a piece is taken off at least nineteen feet in length, so that the ends of the canoe may not be pieced out. A few shorter pieces are wrapped up with the bundle for piecing out the sides.

The Roll

is taken on the back in an upright position, and is carried by a broad band of cedar bark, passing under the lower end of the roll and around in front of the breast and shoulders (**FIG. 4-13**).

Effects of Heat

It is laid where the sun will not shine and harden it. The first effect of heat is to make it pliant. Long exposures to heat or to dry atmosphere makes it hard and brittle.

The Woodwork

is as follows:

Five cross-bars of rock-maple (**FIGS. 4-14, 4-16**, and **4-17**). All the rest is of white cedar, taken from the heart. The sap-wood absorbs water, and would make the canoe too heavy, so it is rejected. The wood requires to be straight and clear, and it is best to use perfectly green wood for the ribs.

Two strips of 16½ feet long, 1½ inch square, tapering toward either end, the ends being notched (see **FIG. 4-14**, A). Each strip is mortised for the cross-bars as follows (see **FIG. 4-17**). The lower outside edge is bevelled off to receive the ends of the ribs.

For dimensions of cross-bars see **FIG. 4-17**. The cross-bars are placed in positions, and the ends of the gunwales are tied with spruce roots after being nailed together to prevent splitting. Each bar is held in place by a peg of hard wood.

For stitching and wrapping, long, slender roots of spruce, or sometimes of elm, are peeled and split in two. Black ash splits are rarely used except for repairing (**FIGS. 4-18, 4-19, 4-20**).

Next (**FIG. 4-14**, B) two strips 1 or 1¼ inch by ½ inch, a little over 19 feet long, to go outside, and (**FIG. 4-14**, C) two top strips, same length, two inches wide in middle, tapering to one inch at either end, 1½ inch thick.

Ribs

About fifty in number (**FIGS. 4-16** and **4-21**) are split with the grain (**FIG. 4-21**, F), so that the heart side of the wood will be on the inner side when the rib is bent. The wood bends better this way. They must be perfectly straight-grained and free from knots. Ribs from the middle are four inches wide, ribs for the ends about three inches wide (**FIG. 4-16** and **FIG. 4-21**, G), and are whittled down to scant half an inch (**FIG. 4-22**). Green wood is generally used, and before it has had any time to season. The ribs may be softened by pouring hot water on them, and should be bent in

FIG. 4-17

FIG. 4-18

FIG. 4-19

FIG. 4-20

FIG. 4-21

pairs to prevent breaking (**FIG. 4-23**). They are held in shape by a band of cedar bark passed around outside.

The ribs are of importance in the shaping of the canoe. The sides bulge out (**FIG. 4-16** and **4-21**). The shape of the ribs determines the depth and stability of the canoe.

Lining Strips

Other strips, an eighth of an inch thick, are carefully whittled out, with straight edges. They are a little over eight feet long, and are designed to be laid inside on the bark, edge to edge, between the bark and ribs. These strips lap an inch or two where they meet, in the middle of the canoe, and are wider here than at the ends, owing to the greater circumference of the canoe in the middle.

Seasoning

Before building all the timber is carefully tied up and laid away. The ribs are allowed to season perfectly, so that they will keep their shape, and not spring back.

The Bed

Next the bed is prepared on a level spot, if possible shaded from the sun. A space is levelled about three and a half feet wide and a little longer than the canoe. The surface is made perfectly smooth. The middle is one or two inches higher than either end.

Building

The frame is laid exactly in the middle of the bed. A small post is driven in the ground (**FIG. 4-24**), on which each end of the frame will rest. Stakes, two or three feet long and about two inches in diameter, are whittled flat on one side, and are driven with the flat side toward the frame at the following points, leaving a space of about a quarter of an inch between the stake and the frame (**FIG. 4-24**), one stake an inch or two on either side of each cross-bar, and another stake half way between each cross-bar. This makes eleven stakes on each side of the frame. Twelve additional stakes are driven as follows: one pair facing each other, at the end of the frame; another pair, an inch apart, about six inches from the last pair, measuring towards the ends of the canoe; and another pair, an inch apart, a foot from these. These last stakes will be nine and a half feet from the middle of the frame, and nineteen feet from the corresponding stakes at the other end. Next, these stakes are all taken up, and the frame laid aside.

FIG. 4-22

To Soften the Bark

Next, the bark is unrolled. If it has laid until it has become a little hardened, it is placed in the river or stream for a day or two. It is spread out flat, and laid upon the bed with the gray or outside surface up. The inside surface is placed downward, and becomes the outside of the canoe.

FIG. 4-23

The frame is replaced upon the bark, so that it will be at the same distance from each side and end of the bed that it was before. At each cross-bar boards are laid across the frame, and heavy stones are laid upon them to keep the frame solid and immovable upon the bark (**FIG. 4-17**, C). The edges of the bark are next bent up in a perpendicular position, and in order that it may bend smoothly slits are made in the bark in an outward direction, at right angles to the frame. A cut is made close to the end of each cross-bar, and one half way between each

bark, which are generally sufficient to allow the bark to be bent up smoothly. As the bark is bent up, the large stakes are slipped back in the holes which they occupied before, and the tops of each

FIG. 4-24

opposite pair are connected with a string of cedar bark which keeps the stakes perfectly perpendicular. At each end it is necessary to take out a small triangular piece or gore, so that the edges can come together without lapping.

Next twenty-two pieces of cedar, one to two feet long, and about ½ or ¾ inch thick, are split out, and whittled thin and flat at one end. This sharpened edge is inserted between the outside edge of the frame and the bent-up bark, opposite each large stake. The other end of the chisel-shaped piece is tightly tied to the large stake outside. By means of the large outside stake and the inside "stake," so-called, the bark is held in a perfectly upright position; and in order to keep the bent-up part more perfectly flat and smooth, the strips of cedar are pushed in lengthwise between the stakes and the bark, on each side of the bark (**FIG. 4-17**, C, and D).

Sometimes, in place of having temporary strips to go on outside the bark, the long outside strip described before is slipped in place instead.

It may now be seen if the bark is not wide enough. If it is not, the sides must be pieced out with a narrow piece, cut in such a way that the eyes in the bark will run in the same direction as those of the large piece.

As a general rule, from the middle to the next bar the strip for piercing is placed on the inside of the large piece, whose upper edge has previously been trimmed straight, and the two are sewed together by stitch shown in **FIG. 4-18**, the spruce root being passed over another root laid along the trimmed-off edge of the large piece of bark to prevent the stitches from tearing out. From the second bar to the end of the canoe, or as far as may be necessary, the strip is placed outside the large piece, and from the second to the end bar is sewed as in **FIG. 4-19**, and from the end bar to the end of the canoe is stitched as in **FIG 4-20**.

Next, the weights are taken off the frame, which is raised up as follows, the bark remaining flat on the bed as before:

A post eight inches long is set up (**FIG. 4-17**, D) one end resting on the bark and the other end supporting either end of the middle cross-bar. Another post, nine inches long, is similarly places under each end of the next cross-bar. Another, twelve inches long, is placed under each end of the end cross-bar; and another, sixteen and a half or seventeen inches, supports each end of the frame.

FIG. 4-25

As the posts are placed under each cross-bar, the weights are replaced; and as these posts are higher at the ends than in the middle, the proper curve is obtained from the gunwales. The temporary strips, that have been placed outside the bent-up portion of the bark, are removed, and the long outside strip before mentioned (**FIG. 4-14**, B) is slipped in place between the outside stakes and the bark. This strip is next nailed to frame with wrought-iron nails that pass through the bark and are clinched on the inside. This outside strip has taken exactly the curve of the frame, but its upper edge, before nailing, was raised so as to be out an eighth of an inch (or the thickness of the bark) higher than the top surface of the frame, so that when the edges of the bark have been bent down, and tacked flat to the frame, a level surface will be presented, upon which the wide top strip will eventually be nailed. Formerly the outer strip was bound to the frame with roots every few inches, but now it is nailed.

FIG. 4-26

FIG. 4-27

The cross-bars are now lashed to the frame, having previously been held only by a peg. The roots are passed through holes in the end of the bars, around the outside strip (see right hand side of **FIG. 4-17**). A two-inch piece of the bark, which has been tacked down upon the frame, is removed at the ends by the cross-bars, where the spruce-roots are to pass around, and the outside strip is cut away to a corresponding extent, so that the roots, when wrapped around, will flush with the surface above.

FIG. 4-28

FIG. 4-29

FIG. 4-30

All the stakes are now removed, and laid away to be ready for the next canoe that may be built, and the canoe taken upside down upon two horses or benches, that will keep the craft clear of the ground.

The shape of the bow is now marked out, either by the eye or with mechanical aid, according to the following rule: A circle, with a radius of seventeen inches, is described (**FIG. 4 -25**), having as a centre a point shown in diagram. The bark is then cut away to this line.

Bowpiece

To stiffen the bow, a bowpiece of cedar, nearly three feet long (**FIG. 4-26**), an inch and a half wide, and half an inch thick on one edge, bevelled and rounded off toward the other edge, is needed. To facilitate bending edgeways it is split into four or five sections (as in **FIG. 4-27**) for about thirty inches. The end that remains unsplit is notched on its thicker edge (**FIG. 4-26**) to receive the lower end of an oval cedar board (**FIG. 4-28**) that is placed upright in the bow underneath the tip of the frame. It is bent to correspond with the curve of the boat, with the thin edge toward the outside of the circle, and wrapped with twine, so that it will keep its shape. The bowpiece is placed between the edges of the bark, which are then sewed together by an over-and-over stitch, which passes through the bowpiece.

A pitch is prepared of rosin and grease, in such proportions that it will neither readily crack in cold water nor melt in the sun. One or the other ingredient is added until by test it is found just right.

Patching and Pitching

The canoe is now placed on the ground, right side up, and all holes are covered on the inside with thin birch bark, that is pasted down with hot pitch. A strip of cloth is saturated with hot pitch, and pressed into the cracks on either side of the bow-piece inside, between the bark and the bowpiece (Fig.**4-29**).

The thin longitudinal strips are next laid in position, edge to edge, lapping several inches by the middle; they are whittled thin here as to lap evenly.

FIG. 4-31

The ribs are next tightly driven in place, commencing at the small end ones, and working toward the middle. The end ribs may be two or three inches apart, being closer toward the middle, where, in many cases they touch. Usually, they are about half an inch apart in the middle. Each rib is driven into place with a square-ended stick and a mallet.

The ends are stuffed with shavings (**FIG. 4-30** and "Section" **FIG. 4-31**), and an oval cedar board is put in the place formerly occupied by the post that supported the end of the frame. The lower end rests in the notch of the bowpiece, while the upper is cut with two shoulders that fit underneath each side of the frame; **FIG. 4-28** shows the cedar board.

FIG. 4-32

The top string is next nailed on to the frame. Almost always a piece of bark, a foot or more long, and nine or ten inches wide, is bent and slipped under, between both top and side strips and the bark. The ends of this piece hang down about three inches below the side strips. The loose ends of the strips are bound together, as in diagram, and the projecting tips of both strips and bowpiece are trimmed off close.

Next, the canoe is turned upside down. If winter bark has been used, the surface is moistened, and the roughness scraped off with a knife. Generally the red rough surface is left in the form of a decorative pattern several inches wide around the upper edge (**FIG. 4-25**). Sometimes the maker's name and date are left in this way.

Finally, a strip of stout canvas, three or four inches wide, is dipped in the melted pitch, and laid on the stitching at the ends, extending up sufficiently far above water line. All cracks and seams are covered with pitch, laid on with a small wooden paddle. While still soft, a wet

FIG. 4-33

FIG. 4-34

finger or the palm of the hand is rubbed over the pitch to smooth it down before it hardens.

Leaks

Water is placed inside, and the leaky places marked, to be stopped when dry. A can of rosin is usually carried in the canoe, and when a leak occurs, the canoe is taken out of the water, the leak discovered by sucking, the place dried with a torch of wood or birch bark, and the pitch applied.

Paddles are made of rock maple, and sometimes of birch and even cedar. Bow paddles are usually longer and narrower in the blade than stern paddles (**FIG. 4-32**).

Bottom Protection

Sometimes the canoe is shod with "shoes," or strings of cedar, laid lengthwise, and tied to the outside of the bark with ash splits that pass through holes in the cedar shoes, and are brought up around the sides of the canoe and tied to each cross-bar. This protects the bottom of the boat from the sharp rocks that abound in some rapid streams.

All canoes are of the general shape of the one described, though this is considerably varied in different localities, some being built with high rolling bows, some slender, some wider, some nearly straight on the bottom, others decidedly curved.

Besides the two paddles the canoe should carry a pole ten feet long, made of a slender spruce, whittled so as to be about one and three-fourths inch in diameter in the middle, and smaller at either end, and having at one end either a ring and a spike or else a pointed cap of iron.

The pole is used for propelling the canoe up swift streams. This, says my informant, "is absolutely indispensable." The person using the pole stands in one end, or nearer the middle if alone, and pushes the canoe along close to the bank, so as to take advantage of the eddies, guiding the canoe with one motion, only to be learned by practice, and keeping the pole usually on the side next to the bank. Where the streams have rocky and pebbly bottoms poling is easy, but in muddy or soft bottoms it is tiresome work.

There is not one man in ten around a boat-house that knows how to handle a shell boat. Frail as these little racing machines are they will last a long time with careful handling.

Now, the same general remarks apply to a birch bark canoe, and careless handling will soon spoil a beautiful craft. **FIGS. 4-33, 4-34, 4-35, 4-36** will show the reader how to pick and carry his boat without injuring it.

FIG. 4-35

A Canvas Canoe

can be made by substituting canvas in the place of birch bark; and if it is kept well painted it makes not only a durable but a very beautiful boat. The writer owns a canvas canoe that is at least fifteen years old and is still in good condition.

About six yards of ten-ounce cotton canvas, fifty inches wide, will be sufficient to cover a canoe, and it will require two papers of four-ounce tinned tacks to secure the canvas on the frame.

The boat should be placed, deck down, upon two "horses" or wooden supports, such as you see carpenters and builders use.

Fold the canvas lengthwise, so as to find the centre, then tack the centre of one side of the cloth to top of bow-piece or stem, using two or three tacks to hold it securely. Stretch

FIG. 4-36

the cloth the length of the boat, pull it taut, with the centre line of the canvas over the keel line of the canoe, and tack the centre of the other end of the cloth to the top of the stern piece.

If care has been taken thus far, an equal portion of the covering will lap the gunwale on each side of the boat.

Begin amidships and drive the tacks, about two inches apart, along the gunwale and an inch below the deck (on the outside). Tack about two feet on one side, pull the cloth tightly across, and tack it about three or four feet on the other side. Continue to alternate, tacking on one side and then the other, until finished.

With the hands and fingers knead the cloth so as to thicken or "full" it where it would otherwise wrinkle, and it will be possible to stretch the canvas without cutting it over the frame.

The cloth that projects beyond gunwale may be used for the deck, or it may be cut off after bringing it over and tacking upon the inside of the gunwale, leaving the canoe open like a birch bark.

The Dug-out

Although not quite as delicate in model or construction as the graceful birch bark canoe, the "dug-out" of the Indians is a most wonderful piece of work, when we consider that it is carved from the solid trunk of a giant tree with the crudest of tools, and is the product of savage labor.

Few people now living have enjoyed the opportunity of seeing one built, and, as the author is not numbered among that select few, he considers it a privilege to be able to quote the following interesting account given by Mr. J. H. Mallett, of Helena.

How to Build a Siwash Canoe

"While visiting one of the small towns along Puget Sound, I was greatly interested in the way the Indians built their canoes. It is really wonderful how these aborigines can, with the crudest means and with a few days' work, convert an unwieldy log into a trim and pretty canoe.

"One morning I saw a buck building a fire at the base of a large cedar-tree, and he told me that this was the first step in the construction of a canoe that he intended to use upon the following Saturday. He kept the fire burning merrily all that day and far into the night, when a wind came up and completed the downfall of the monarch of the forest. The next day the man arose betimes, and, borrowing a cross-cut saw from a logger, cut the trunk of the tree in twain at a point some fifteen feet from where it had broken off, and then with a dull hatchet he hacked away until the log had assumed the shape of the desired canoe. In this work he was helped by his squaw. The old fellow then built a fire on the upper part of the log, guiding the course of the fire with daubs of clay, and in due course of time the interior of the canoe had been burned out. Half a day's work with the hatchet rendered the inside smooth and shapely.

"The canoe was now, I thought, complete, though it appeared to be dangerously narrow of beam. This the Indian soon remedied. He filled the shell two-thirds full of water, and into the fluid he dropped half a dozen stones that had been heating in the fire for nearly a day. The water at once attained a boiling point, and so softened the wood that the buck and squaw were enabled to draw out the sides and thus supply the necessary breadth of beam. Thwarts and slats were then placed in the canoe, and the water and stones thrown out. When the steamed wood began to cool and contract the thwarts held it back, and the sides held thwarts, and here the canoe was complete, without a nail, joint, or crevice, for it was made of one piece of wood. The Siwash did not complete it as soon as he had promised, but it only took him eight days."

The Scow

There can be but few boys who are not familiar with that large and useful tribe of flat-bottomed, perpendicular-sided boats called "scows." These crafts are used as coal barges, lighters, flat-boats, sail-boats, and

FIG. 4-37

Side Board

row-boats; but it is only to the construction of the last named class that this chapter will be devoted.

To build a scow-shaped row-boat is not a difficult feat, even for a boy; and when it is finished he will find it to be a very convenient boat, roomy, and not hard to row.

The material necessary consists of eight or ten three-quarter-inch pine boards, one one-inch board, some fivepenny nails, and about a half pound of wrought-iron nails of the same size as the ones just mentioned.

FIG. 4-38

A saw, a plane, and a sharp hatchet are requisite in the way of tools. Other tools, if not absolutely necessary, should not on that account be ignored, as they may come in very handy at times.

When selecting the lumber for the boat, pick out those pieces which are free from large knots and other blemishes. Reserve two of the best boards for the sides, and let them measure 11 feet in length and 12 inches in width when trimmed. Measuring toward the centre, mark a point 2½ feet from each end of one of the side boards upon the edge

FIG. 4-39

selected for the bottom. Measuring from the bottom edge toward the top, mark a point upon each end 8 inches from the bottom. Saw off the triangular pieces between these points (**FIG. 4-37**). Round off the angles with a plane, and make the other side board an exact duplicate of the one just described (**FIG. 4-38**).

For the ends of the boat use the 1½-inch plank, making of it two small boards to fit between the ends of the side boards.

The side pieces now measure 4 inches upon each end (**FIG. 4-37**), hence the end boards ought to be 4 inches wide; but to make sure of neat

joints, it is best to allow
½ inch extra. Make the
end pieces 3 feet long, 4½
inches wide, and 1 inch
thick. Set the side pieces
parallel to each other
upon their straight or top
edges, and between their
ends fit the end boards
(**FIG. 4-38**). After seeing

that all the corners are square, nail the end boards in place. Plane off
the protruding edges at the bow and stern, so that the bottom pieces
overlapping them will make close joints; then nail the bottom boards
on crosswise, as shown in the illustration (**FIG. 4-39**). All nails must
be driven in so that their heads are below the surface of the board, or
as carpenters call it, countersunk, and the indentations made should
be puttied up.

Turn the scow over, and upon the inside, at the middle of the bottom, nail a ¾-inch long bottom board (**FIGS. 4-40** and **4-41**). Next cut
two small boards of ¾-inch plank; make them 7 inches wide and about
1 foot 5 inches long; cut out a place in one end of each, as shown by A,
FIG. 4-40; these are to serve as rowlocks, and should be nailed with
wrought-iron nails to the inside of the boat, so that the centres of the
rowlocks are about 4 feet 10 inches from the end which will be the stern
of the boat; this is the sim-
plest style of rowlock, but
a much neater one can be
made by using thole-pins
(**FIG. 4-41**, B).

Turn the boat upon its
side and nail a strip 11
feet long, 2 inches wide,
and 1 inch thick upon the
upper edge of the side

Thole-pin

board; repeat the operation on the other side, using wrought nails and clinching them. If thole-pins are intended to be used, before nailing the strips upon the sides, 4 feet 9 inches from one end of each strip cut a notch in the side ½ inch deep and 1½ wide; 3 inches from this notch, or 5 feet from the same end, cut another similar notch. When these strips are nailed on the sides (**FIG. 4-41**) the notches cut in them form the rowlocks. Put in more nails near the rowlocks than elsewhere, to help to withstand the greater strain that that part has to bear. The end of the boat nearest the rowlocks is the stern. Of oak or some hard wood make four thole-pins to fit into the rowlocks (**FIG. 4-41**, B).

For a seat use a board about 1 foot wide; it should be 3 feet long to fit inside the boat; the seat rests upon two cleats set 6 inches below the top of the side boards (**FIG. 4-41**); the aft edge of the seat should be about 1 foot forward of the rowlocks.

A bow and stern seat should be made for passengers; these seats need not set so low as the one occupied by the oarsman, and may be made of boards nailed across the top of the boat at the bow and stern, and the space underneath them may be used for lockers.

If a chain "painter" is used, fasten it to the bow with an iron staple (**FIG. 4-40**); but if a rope is preferred, or is more easily obtained, run one end of it through a hole bored for the purpose in the bow seat, and knot the end so that it cannot slip out (**FIG. 4-41**). When such a boat is built with clean, close-fitting joints, and the cracks daubed with thick paint, it is often unnecessary to do any further caulking. A good method is to saturate pieces of woollen cloth with paint and place them between the different parts before they are joined. After the carpenter work is done, go to the paint shop and get a can of white paint, first telling the painter to weigh the can. After you have used what paint is necessary, return the can, have it weighed, and pay only for the amount used. If you are well known the painter will not hesitate to allow you to do this, and you will find it the most economical way. After the first coat of paint is dry put on a second coat; as soon as that is hardened, which will be in two or three days, according to the weather, your boat is ready for launching; it may leak at first, but after the seams have swelled it will be almost perfectly dry inside.

A Floating Camp,
or the Boy's Own Flat-Boat

Flat-boats are essentially inland craft, having their origin with the birth of trade in the West before the puffing and panting steam-boats plowed their way through the turbid waters of Western rivers. They are craft that can be used on any stream large enough to float a yawl, but the St. John's River, Florida, is perhaps the most tempting stream for the amateur flat-boatman. The numerous inlets and lakes connected with the river, the luxuriant semi-tropical foliage on the banks, the strange-looking fish and great, stupid alligators, the beautiful white herons and hundreds of water-fowl of many descriptions—all form features that add interest to its navigation and inducements to hunters, fishermen, naturalists, and pleasure-seekers scarcely equalled by any other accessible river of the United States.

To build the hull of the flat-boat, use pine lumber. For the sides select two good, straight 2-inch planks, 14 feet long and about 16 inches wide. Take one of the planks (**FIG. 4-42**), measure 6 inches from the top upon each end, and mark the points A, a (**FIG. 4-42**); then upon the bottom measure from each end toward the centre 2 feet, and mark the points B, b (**FIG. 4-42**). Saw off the corners A, B and a, b, and round the angles in the

FIG. 4-42

manner described on page 52 and illustrated by **FIG. 4-38**. Next take two 2-inch planks, 6½ inches wide and 6 feet long, for the stem and stern; set the side pieces on edge upside down, and nail on the two end pieces (see **FIG. 4-43**). Then, allowing 4 inches—the thickness of the two sides—there will be a space inside the boat of 5 feet 8 inches. Take three pieces of scantling about 3 inches thick and 5 feet 8 inches long; place one near the end flush with the bottom of the boat just where the sheer of bow and stern begins (see A and B, **FIG. 4-43**). After fitting them carefully, nail them firmly. Nail the other piece of scantling in place at the point C (**FIG. 4-43**), so that it will measure 6 feet from the outside of the brace A to the outside of the brace C. Plane off the protruding edges of the bow and stern.

FIG. 4-43

FIG. 4-44

A bottom may now be put on as described on page 52 and illustrated by **FIG. 4-39**, or a regular flat-boat bottom can be made by selecting good, straight 1/2-inch lumber a little over 14 feet long, to allow for the curve.

Nail an end of one of the bottom boards to the stern board (see **FIG. 4-44**); its side edge must be flush with the outer edge of the side piece. Bend the bottom board carefully along the curve to the first cross piece A (**FIG. 4-44**) and nail it firmly; nail it again at C and at the bow, being careful to make it conform to the curve of the sides. Follow the same plan with the next board, keeping it close up against the first board so as to leave no crack when the bottom is finished. Caulk up any accidental cracks with oakum; give the whole hull a coating of coal tar, and allow it to harden. The remainder of the work is comparatively easy.

After the coal tar has hardened, turn the boat over and erect four posts, one at each end of the cross piece A and one at each end of the cross piece C (**FIG. 4-43** or **4-44**).

The tops of the posts for this size boat should be about 3½ feet above the bottom of the hull. Put a cross piece on the top of the post at A and another at C, and the framework of your cabin is done. It may now be covered with canvas, or, as in the illustrations, with thin planks, in which case make the roof of ¼-inch boards, bending them in an arch so that the middle will rise about one foot higher than the sides.

The eaves should over-hang about six inches beyond the cabin upon each side.

Board up the sides with the same material used for the roofing, leaving openings for windows and doors. Pieces of shoe leather make very good hinges for the door, but iron hinges are of course the best. The cabin can then be floored, a bunk or two may be built, and as many other conveniences as your taste or necessities may indicate, can be provided, a few clothes hooks, etc.

FIG. 4-45

Side View of Flat-Boat

Put in rowlocks; those used in the Crusoe raft are best for large flat-boats, but for this one make rowlocks on the same plan as the ones illustrated by **FIG. 4-40**, A (page 53). There should be three rowlocks, one for the steering oar and two near the front for rowing (see **FIG. 4-43**).

Set a seat in front of the rowlock with a hole in it for the "jack-staff" to pass through. The jack-staff should be made so that it can be taken out and put in at pleasure. This can be done by making a simple socket underneath the seat for the end of the staff to fit in.

The flat-boat is now ready to be launched, which should be done with appropriate ceremonies. **FIG. 4-46** shows the side view of a 14-foot flat-boat; the cabin, to better show its construction, is increased in height in the drawing, and, according to the scale, it measures about five feet at the sides and six feet at the ridge-pole. **FIG. 4-46** shows a front view of the same.

FIG. 4-46

Front View of Flat-Boat

FIG. 4-47

Top View of Flat-Boat

FIG. 4-48

Perspective View of Interior of a Cabin

FIG. 4-47 shows a top view of a flat-boat as it would appear looking down upon the roof of the cabin.

The large diagram (**FIG. 4-48**) drawn in perspective shows how a cabin for a little larger boat can be arranged. The diagram is drawn on the scale of feet marked below it. The floor is about six feet long by six feet wide, and the side walls are five feet high. A cabin of these dimensions can be arranged with four folding berths, two upon each side, made of boards each two feet wide and fastened to the sides by hinges. The top berths may be supported by their hinges and a cross beam upon the inside, and by two broad straps upon the outside; the straps button on to knobs in the ends of the berths. The lower berths can be provided with folding legs, as shown by the illustration (**FIG. 4-48**), which shows two berths down on the left-hand side and two folded up on the right-hand side. The lockers underneath the bottom berths can be used for storing away bed-clothes.

In the rear, under a looking-glass, can be seen a device for a folding desk, which is simply a square board attached to the wall, like the berths, by hinges, and which may be let down so as to hang flat against the wall, out of the way when the berths are to be used. The legs to the desk are hinged at the bottom, and as the desk is raised the legs fall forward, resting against the cleat upon the bottom of the top board, which holds it in the position shown by the diagram. Many other little conveniences may be added, such as a small cooking-stove, book-shelves, gun-racks, etc., but I shall not go into further details, my aim being only to suggest how it may be done, as every boy who is smart enough to build a flat-boat will have his own peculiar ideas about the manner in which it should be fitted up inside. The interior construction depends, in a measure, upon the number of persons who are to occupy the cabin, and whether it is to be used by a party of young naturalists upon a collecting tour, or for fishing and shooting excursions, or simply as a sort of picnic boat for a few days' enjoyment, such as most boys in the country are quite well able to plan and carry out unaided.

Although a rude home-made flat-boat does not possess speed, yet with a square sail rigged on the jack-staff, and with a good wind over the stern, it will make good time; and as this sort of craft draws only a few inches of water, it can float in creeks and inlets where a well-loaded row-boat would drag bottom.

The advantages of a flat-boat consist in the fact that it is a comfortable, cosey little house in which one could spend a month very pleasantly hunting or fishing, or visiting the various points of interest along the shores of the river and inlets, and, whenever the floating home drifts in sight of a pleasant place to stop, all that is necessary is to make fast to the bank, thus escaping the nuisance of moving bag and baggage.

During a cruise the members of the party will have frequent occasion to put in practice all manner of devices for saving labor, and making the hunter as far as possible independent of a mate when, as often happens, two boys cannot be spared from the boat to go foraging together. One of

FIG. 4-49

these "wrinkles," as they are termed, is a floating fish-car, adapted for minnows or large fish, which being fastened to the fisherman's waist, floats behind as he wades. This arrangement not only saves much weariness in carrying finny spoils to camp after, perhaps, a long and trying day, but it helps to keep the fish fresh; and when not in active use it may be towed behind "The Ark."

Many hints of this same kind might be given, but this one will suffice to show that a boy with his wits about him can lighten very materially the fatigues inseparable from camping out and flat-boating. Endurance of hardship is noble in itself, and there is call enough for it in this rough-and-tumble world; but the fellow who most enjoys "roughing it" in a trip outdoors is he who is quickest to save himself unnecessary exertion by using the simplest means at hand.

The Yankee Pine

From the saw-mills away up among the tributaries of the Ohio River come floating down to the towns along the shore great rafts of pine lumber. These rafts are always objects of interest to the boys, for the youngsters know that when moored to the shore the solidly packed planks make a splendid platform to swim from. Fine springing-boards can be made of the projecting blades of the gigantic sweeps which are used to guide the mammoth rafts, and, somewhere aboard, there is always to be found a "Yankee Pine." Just when or why this style of skiff was dubbed with such a peculiar name I am unable to state; but this I know, that when a raft is to be broken up and carted away to the lumber yards there is, or always used to be, a good, light skiff to be had cheap.

However, all boys do not live on the bank of the river, and if they did there would hardly be "Yankee Pines" enough to go round; so we will at once proceed to see how to build one for ourselves. Although my readers may find the "Yankee Pine" a little more difficult to build than the blunt-ended, flat-bottomed scow, it really is a comparatively simple piece of work for boys familiar with the use of carpenters' tools.

For the side pieces select two straight-grained pine boards free from knots. These boards should be about 13 or 14 feet long, a couple of inches over a foot in width, and as nearly alike as possible in texture. Besides these, there should be in the neighborhood of a dozen other ¾-inch planks, an inch or two over a half foot in width. A small piece of 2-inch plank for the stern piece is also necessary. Upon the bottom edge of the side board measure off from each end toward the centre 4 inches, mark the points, and saw off the corners shown by the dotted line in **FIG. 4-49**. Next take a piece of board 4 feet long and a foot wide, saw off the corners as you did on the side board, making it 4 feet on the top and 3 feet 4 inches on the bottom. This board is to be used only as a centre brace while modelling the boat.

Out of the 2-inch plank make a stern piece of the same shape as the centre brace; let it be 1 foot wide, 14 inches long on the bottom, and 20 inches long on top. Set the side boards on their shorter or bottom edges, and place the centre brace in the middle, as shown by **FIG. 4-50**; nail the side boards to it, using only enough nails to hold temporarily. Draw the side boards together at the bow, and against the stern board at the stern (**FIG. 4-50**). Hold the side pieces in position by the means of ropes. A stem should be ready to fix in the bow (**FIG. 4-51**). This had better be a few inches longer than the sides are broad, as it is a simple matter to saw off the top after it is fitted. Make the stem of a triangular piece of timber, by planning off the front edge until a flat surface about ½ inch broad is obtained; 2 inches from the front, upon each side, cut a groove just the thickness of the side boards (¾ inch). Trim the stem so that the side pieces at the bow fit the grooves snugly, and nail the side boards to the stem and to the stern piece (**FIG. 4-50**).

FIG. 4-50

FIG. 4-51

Turn the boat upside down, and it will be discovered that the outlines of the bottom form an arch from stem to stern. If left in this shape the boat will sink too deep amidships. Remedy the defect by planing the bottom edge of both side pieces, reducing the convex form to straight lines in the middle. This will allow the bow and stern to sheer, but at the same time will make the central part of the bottom flat, and by having less to drag through the water make it easier to row. Nail the bottom boards on crosswise, and as, on account of the form of the boat, no two boards will be of the same size, they must be first nailed on and the projecting ends sawed off afterward. The centre brace may now be taken out and a long bottom board nailed to the centre of the bottom upon the inside of the boat (**FIG. 4-51**). Cut a small cross piece (B, **FIG. 4-52**) so that it will fit across the bow 3 inches below the top of the side boards. Nail it in place, driving the nails from the outside of the sideboard through and into the end of the stick B. Saw out a bow seat, and, allowing the broad end to rest on the cross stick B, fit the seat in and secure it with nails (**FIG. 4-52**); 3 inches below the top of the stern piece nail a cleat across. At the same distance below the side board put a cross stick similar to the one in the bow. This and the cleat on the stern piece form rests for the stern seat. Five feet from the stern, saw a notch 2 inches deep and 1½ inch long in each side board (A, A', **FIG. 4-52**). Saw two more notches of the same size 3 inches from the first; these will make the rowlock when the side strips have been fastened on.

FIG. 4-52

These strips should each be made of 1-inch plank, 2 inches wide and an inch or two longer than the side boards. Nail the strips on the outside of the boat flush with the top of the side boards, making a neat joint at the stern piece, as shown in the illustration (**FIG. 4-52**). Cut two short strips to fit upon the inside at the rowlocks, and fasten them firmly on with screws (**FIG. 4-52**, A). Next cut two cleats for the oarsman's seat to rest upon. Nail them to the side boards amidship a little nearer the bottom than the top, so that the seat, when resting upon the cleats, will be about half the distance from the top edge to the bottom of the side boards. Let the aft end of the cleats be about 6 feet 2 inches from the stern. Make thole-pins of some hard wood to fit in the rowlocks, like those heretofore described and illustrated by **FIG. 4-41**, B, page 53.

FIG. 4-53

The Yankee Pine now only needs a keel board to complete it. This must be placed exactly in the centre, and is fastened on by a couple of screws at the thin end and nails from the inside of the boat. It is also fastened to the upright stick at the stern by screws (**FIG. 4-53**).

If the joints have been carefully made, your Yankee Pine is now ready for launching. Being made of rough lumber it needs no paint or varnish, but is a sort of rough-and-ready affair, light to row; and it ought to float four people with ease. By using planed pine or cedar lumber, and with hard-wood stem and stern, a very pretty row-boat can be made upon the same plan as a Yankee Pine, or by putting in a centre-board and "stepping" a mast in the bow, the Yankee Pine can be transformed into a sail-boat. But before experimenting in this line of boat building, the beginner had better read the following chapter on how to rig and sail small boats.

FIG. 4-54

Top View of "Man Friday"

CHAPTER 5

HOW TO
RIG AND SAIL
SMALL
BOATS

How to Sail a Boat

To have the tiller in one's own hands and feel competent, under all ordinary circumstances, to bring a boat safely into port, gives the same zest and excitement to a sail (only in a far greater degree) that the handling of the whip and reins over a lively trotter does to a drive.

Knowing and feeling this, it was my intention to devote a couple of chapters to telling how to sail a boat; but through the kind courtesy of the editor of *The American Canoeist,* I am able to do much better by giving my readers a talk on this subject by one whose theoretical knowledge and practical experience renders him pre-eminently fit to give reliable advice and counsel. The following is what Mr. Charles Ledyard Norton, editor of the above-mentioned journal, says:

"Very many persons seem to ignore the fact that a boy who knows how to manage a gun is, upon the whole, less likely to be shot than one who is a bungler through ignorance, or that a good swimmer is less likely to be drowned than a poor one. Such, however, is the truth beyond question. If a skilled sportsman is now and then shot, or an expert swimmer drowned, the fault is not apt to be his own, and if the one who is really to blame had received proper training, it is not likely that the accident would have occurred at all. The same argument holds good with regard to the management of boats, and the author is confident that he merits the thanks of mothers, whether he receives them or not, for giving their boys a few hints as to practical rigging and sailing.

"In general, there are three ways of learning how to sail boats. First, from the light of nature, which is a poor way; second, from books, which is better; and third, from another fellow who knows how, which is best of all. I will try to make this article as much like the other fellow and as little bookish as possible.

"Of course, what I shall say in these few paragraphs will be of small use to those who live within reach of the sea or some big lake, and have always been used to boats; but there are thousands and thousands of boys and men who never saw the sea, nor even set eyes on a sail, and who have not the least idea how to make the wind take them where they want to go. I once knew some young men from the interior who went down to the sea-side and hired a boat, with the idea that they had nothing to do but hoist the sail and be blown wherever they liked. The result was that they performed a remarkable set of manœuvres within sight of the boat-house, and at last went helplessly out to sea and had to be sent after and brought back, when they were well laughed at for their performances, and had reason to consider themselves lucky for having gotten off so cheaply.

"The general principles of sailing are as simple as the national game of 'one ole cat.' That is to say, if the wind always blew moderately and steadily, it would be as easy and as safe to sail a boat as it is to drive a steady old family horse of good and regular habits. The fact, however, is that winds and currents are variable in their moods, and as capable of unexpected freaks as the most fiery of unbroken colts; but when properly watched and humored they are tractable and fascinating playmates and servants.

"Now, let us come right down to first principles. Take a bit of pine board, sharpen it at one end, set up a mast

FIG. 5-1

about a quarter of the length of the whole piece from the bow, fit on a square piece of stiff paper or card for a sail, and you are ready for action. Put this in the water, with the sail set squarely across (A, **FIG. 5-1**), and she will run off before the wind—which is supposed to be blowing as indicated by the arrow—at a good rate of speed. If she does not steer herself, put a small weight near the stern, or square end; or, if you like, arrange a thin bit of wood for a rudder.

FIG. 5-2

"Probably the first primeval man who was born with nautical instincts discovered this fact, and, using a bush for a sail, greatly astonished his fellow primevals by winning some prehistoric regatta. But that was all he could do. He was as helpless as a balloonist is in mid-air. He could go, but he could not get back, and we may be sure that ages passed away before the possibility of sailing to windward was discovered.

"Now, put up, or 'step,' another mast and sail like the first, about as far from the stern as the first is from the bow. Turn the two sails at an angle of forty-five degrees across the boat (B or C, **FIG. 5-1**), and set her adrift. She will make considerable progress across the course of the wind, although she will at the same time drift with it. If she wholly refuses to go in the right direction, place a light weight on her bow, so that she will be a little 'down by the head,' or move the aftermost mast and sail a little nearer to the stern.

"The little rude affair thus used for experiment will not actually make any progress to windward, because she is so light that she moves sidewise almost as easily as she does forward. With a larger, deeper boat, and with sails which can be set at any angle, the effect will be different. So long as the wind presses against the after side of the sail, the boat will move through the water in the direction of the least resistance, which is forward. A square sail, having the mast in the middle, was easiest to begin with for purposes of explanation; but now we will change to a 'fore-and-aft' rig—that is, one with the mast at the forward edge or 'luff' of the sail, as in **FIG. 5-2** Suppose the sail to be set at the angle shown, and the wind blowing as the arrow points. The boat cannot readily move sidewise, because of the broadside resistance; she does not move backward, because the wind is pressing on the aftermost side of the sail. So she very naturally moves forward. When she nears buoy No. I, the helmsman moves the 'tiller,' or handle of the rudder, toward the sail. This causes the boat to turn her head toward buoy No. 2, the sail swings across to the other side of the boat and fills on that side, which now in turn becomes the aftermost, and she moves toward buoy No. 2 nearly at right angles to her former course. Thus, through a series of zig-zags, the wind is made to work against itself. This operation is called 'tacking,' or 'working to windward,' and the act of turning, as at the buoys No. 1 and No. 2, is called 'going about.'

"It will be seen, then, that the science of sailing lies in being able to manage a boat with her head pointing at any possible angle to or from the wind. Nothing but experience can teach one all the niceties of the art, but a little aptitude and address will do to start with, keeping near shore and carrying little sail.

Simplest Rig Possible

"I will suppose that the reader has the use of a broad, flat-bottomed boat without any rudder. (See **FIG. 5-3**.) She cannot be made to work like a racing yacht under canvas, but lots of fun can be had out of her.

"Do not go to any considerable expense at the outset. Procure an old sheet, or an old hay-cover, six or eight feet square, and experiment with that before spending your money on new material. If it is a sheet, and somewhat weakly in its texture, turn all the edges in and sew them, so that it shall not give way at the hems. At each corner sew on a few inches of strong twine, forming loops at the angles. Sew on, also, eyelets or small loops along the edge which is intended for the luff of the sail, so that it can be laced to the mast.

"You are now ready for your spars, namely, a mast and a 'sprit,' the former a couple of feet longer than the luff of the sail, and the latter to be cut off when you find how long you want it. Let these spars be of pine, or spruce, or bamboo—as light as possible, especially the sprit. An inch and a half diameter will do for the mast, and an inch and a quarter for the sprit, tapering to an inch at the top. To 'step' the mast, bore a hole through one of the thwarts (seats) near the bow, and make a socket or step on the bottom of the boat, just under the aforesaid hole—or if anything a trifle farther forward—to receive the foot of the mast. This will hold the mast upright, or with a slight 'rake' aft.

FIG. 5-3

"Lace the luff of the sail to the mast so that its lower edge will swing clear by a foot or so of the boat's sides. Make fast to the loop at D a stout line, ten or twelve feet long. This is called the 'sheet,' and gives control of the sail. The upper end of the sprit, C, E, is trimmed so that the loop at C will fit over it but not slip down. The lower end is simply notched to receive a short line called a 'snotter,' as shown in the detailed drawing at the right of the cut (**FIG. 5-3**). It will be readily understood that, when the sprit is pushed upward in the direction of C, the sail will stand spread out. The line is placed in the notch at E and pulled up until the sail sets properly, when it is made fast to a cleat or to a cross piece at F. This device is in common use and has its advantages, but a simple loop for the foot of the sprit to rest in is more easily made and will do nearly as well. H is an oar for steering. Having thus described the simplest rig possible, we may turn our attention to more elegant and elaborate but not always preferable outfits.

Leg-of-Mutton Rig

"One of the prettiest and most convenient rigs for a small boat is known as the 'leg-of-mutton sharpie rig' (**FIG. 5-4**). The sail is triangular, and the sprit, instead of reaching to its upper corner, stands nearly at right angles to the mast. It is held in position at the mast by the devices already described. This

Leg of-mutton Rig

FIG. 5-4

FIG. 5-5

A New Device

rig has the advantage of keeping the whole sail flatter than any others for the end of the sprit cannot 'kick up,' as the phrase goes, and so the sail holds all the wind it receives.

"**FIG. 5-5** shows a device, published for the first time in the *St. Nicholas Magazine* for September, 1880, which enables the sailor to step and unstep his mast, and hoist or lower his sail without leaving his seat—a matter of great importance when the boat is light and tottlish, as in the case of that most beautiful of small craft, the modern canoe, where the navigator sits habitually amidships. The lower mast (A, B, **FIG. 5-5**) stands about two and a half feet above the deck. It is fitted at the head with a metal ferrule and pin, and just above the deck with two half-cleats or other similar devices (A). The topmast (C, D) is fitted at F with a stout ring, and has double halyards (E) rove through or around its foot. The lower mast (see lower part of **FIG. 5-5**), the canoeist desiring to make sail brings the boat's head to the wind, takes the top-mast with the sail loosely furled in one hand, and the halyards in the other. It is easy for him by raising this mast, without leaving his seat, to pass the halyards one on each side of the lower mast and let them fall into place close to the deck under the half-cleats at A. Then, holding the halyards taut enough to keep them in position, he will hook the topmast ring over the pin in the lower mast-head and haul away (see top part of **FIG. 5-5**).

The mast will rise into place, where it is made fast. A collar of leather, or a knob of some kind, placed on the top-mast just below the ring, will act as a fulcrum when the halyards are hauled taut, and keep the mast from working to and fro.

"The advantages of the rig are obvious. The mast can be raised without standing up, and in case of necessity the halyards can be let go and the mast and sail unshipped and stowed below with the greatest ease and expedition, leaving only the short lower mast standing. A leg-of-mutton sail with a common boom along the foot is shown in the cut as the most easily illustrated application of the device, but there is no reason why it may not be applied to a sail of different shape, with a sprit instead of a boom, and a square instead of a pointed head.

The Latteen Rig

is recommended only for boats which are 'stiff'—not tottlish, that is. The fact that a considerable portion of the sail projects forward of the mast renders it awkward in case of a sudden shift of wind. Its most convenient form is shown in **FIG. 5-6**. The arrangement for shipping and unshipping the yard is precisely like that shown in **FIG. 5-5**—a short lower mast with a pin at the top and a ring fitted to the yard. It has a boom at the foot which is joined to the yard at C by means of a hook or a simple lashing, having sufficient play to allow the two spars to shut up together like a pair of dividers. The boom (C, E) has, where it meets the short lower mast, a half-cleat or jaw, shown in detail at the bottom of the cut (**FIG. 5-6**), the circle representing a cross-section of the mast. This should be lashed to the boom, as screws or bolts would weaken it. To take in sail, the boatman brings the boat to the wind, seizes the boom and draws it toward him. This disengages it from the mast. He then shoves it forward, when the yard (C, D) falls of its own weight into his hands, and can be at once lifted clear of the lower mast. To keep the sail flat, it is possible to arrange a collar on the lower

FIG. 5-6

The Latteen Rig

mast so that the boom, when once in position, cannot slip upward and suffer the sail to bag.

The Cat-Rig

so popular on the North Atlantic coast, is indicated in **FIG. 5-2**. The spar at the head of the sail is called a 'gaff,' and, like the boom, it fits the mast with semicircular jaws. The sail is hoisted and lowered by means of halyards rove through a block near the mast-head. The mast is set in the bows—'chock up in the eyes of her,' as a sailor would say. A single leg-of-mutton sail will not work in this position, because the greater part of its area is too far forward of amidships. No rig is handier or safer than this in working to windward; but off the wind—running before, or nearly before it, that is—the weight of mast and sail, and the pressure of the wind at one side and far forward, make the boat very difficult and dangerous to steer. Prudent boatmen often avoid doing so by keeping the wind on the quarter and, as it were, tacking to leeward.

"This suggests the question of 'jibing,' an operation always to be avoided if possible. Suppose the wind to be astern, and the boat running nearly before it. It becomes necessary to change your course toward the side on which the sail is drawing. The safest way is to turn at first in the opposite direction, put the helm 'down' (toward the sail), bring the boat up into the wind, turn her entirely around, and stand off on the new tack. This, however, is not always possible. Hauling in the sheet until the sail fills on the other side is 'jibing;' but when this happens it goes over with a rush that sometimes carries mast and sheet or upsets the boat; hence the operation should be first undertaken in a light wind. It is necessary to know how to do it, for sometimes a sail insists upon jibing very unexpectedly, and it is best to be prepared for such emergencies.

How to Make a Sail

"For the sails of such boats as are considered in this paper, there is no better material than unbleached twilled cotton sheeting. It is to be had two and a half or even three yards wide. In cutting out your sail, let the selvedge be at the 'leech,' or aftermost edge. This, of course, makes it necessary to cut the luff and foot 'bias,' and they are very likely to stretch in the making, so that the sail will assume a different shape from what was intended. To avoid this, baste the hem carefully before sewing, and 'hold in' a little to prevent fulling. It is a good plan to tack the material on the floor before cutting, and mark the outline of the sail with pencil. Stout tape stitched along the bias edges will make a sure thing of it, and the material can be cut, making due allowance for the hem. Better take feminine advice on this process. The hems should be half an inch deep all around, selvedge and all, and it will do no harm to reinforce them with cord if you wish to make a thoroughly good piece of work.

"For running-rigging, nothing is better than laid or braided-cotton cord, such as is used for awnings and sash-cords. If this is not easily procured, any stout twine will answer. It can be doubled and twisted as often as necessary. The smallest manila rope is rather stiff and unmanageable for such light sails as ours.

"In fitting out a boat of any kind, iron, unless galvanized, is to be avoided as much as possible, on account of its liability to rust. Use brass or copper instead.

Hints to Beginners

"Nothing has been said about reefing thus far, because small boats under the management of beginners should not be afloat in a 'reefing breeze.' Reefing is the operation of reducing the spread of sail when the wind becomes too fresh. If you will look at **FIG. 5-6** you will see rows of short marks on the sail above the boom. These are 'reef-points'—bits of line about a foot long passing through holes in the sail, and knotted so that they will not slip. In reefing, the sail is lowered and that portion of it between the boom and the reef-points is gathered together, and the points are tied around both it and the boom. When the lower row of points is used it is a single reef. Both rows together are a double reef.

"Make your first practical experiment *with a small sail and with the wind blowing toward the shore.* Row out a little way, and then sail in any direction in which you can make the boat go, straight back to shore if you can, with the sail out nearly at right angles with the boat. Then try running along shore with the sheet hauled in a little, and the sail on the side nearest the shore. You will soon learn what your craft can do, and will probably find that she will make very little, if any, head-way to windward. This is partly because she slides sidewise over the water. To prevent it you may use a 'lee-board'—namely, a broad board hung over the side of the boat (G, **FIG. 5-3**). This must be held by stout lines, as the strain upon it is very heavy. It should be placed a little forward of the middle of the boat. It must be on the side away from the wind—the lee side—and must be shifted when you go about. Keels and centre-boards are permanent contrivances for the same purpose, but a lee-board answers very well as a makeshift, and is even used habitu-ally by some canoeists and other boatmen.

"In small boats it is sometimes desirable to sit amidships, because sitting in the stern raises the bow too high out of water; steering may be done with an oar over the lee side, or with 'yoke-lines' attached to a cross piece on the rudder-head, or even to the tiller. In this last case, the lines must be rove through rings or pulleys at the sides of the boat opposite the end of the tiller. When the handle of the oar (H, **FIG. 5-3**)—or the tiller (F, **FIG. 5-6**) if a rudder is used—is pushed to the right, the boat will turn to the left, and *vice versâ.* The science of steering consists in knowing when to push and how much to push—very simple, you see, in the statement, but not always so easy in practice.

"The sail should be so adjusted in relation to the rest of the boat that, when the sheet is hauled close in and made fast, the boat, if left to herself, will point her head to the wind like a weather-cock, and drift slowly astern. If it is found that the sail is so far forward that she will not do this, the fault may be remedied by stepping the mast further aft, or by rigging a small sail near the stern. This is called a 'dandy,' or 'steering-sail,' and is especially convenient in a boat whose size or arrangement necessitates sitting amidships. It may be rigged like the mainsail, and when its sheet is once made fast will ordinarily take care of itself in tacking.

"Remember that, if the wind freshens or a squall strikes you, the position of safety is with the boat's head to the wind. When in doubt what to do, push the helm down (toward the sail) and haul in the slack of the sheet as the boat comes up into the wind. If she is moving astern, or will not mind her helm—and of course she will not if she is not moving—pull her head around to the wind with an oar, and experiment cautiously until you find which way you can make her go.

"In making a landing, always calculate to have the boat's head as near the wind as possible when she ceases to move. This whether you lower your sail or not.

"Thus, if the wind is offshore, as shown at A, Fig. 5-7, land at F or G, with the bow toward the shore. If the wind is from the direction of B, land at E with the bow toward B, or at F; if at the latter, the boom will swing away from the wharf and permit you to lie alongside. If the wind is from D, reverse these positions. If the wind comes from the direction of C, land either at F or G, with the bow pointing off shore.

FIG. 5-7

"If you have no one to tell you what to do, you will have to feel your way slowly and learn by experience; but if you have nautical instincts you will soon make your boat do what you wish her to do as far as she is able. *But first learn to swim before you try to sail a boat.*"

Volumes have been written on the subject treated in these few pages, and it is not yet exhausted. The hints here given are safe ones to follow, and will, it is hoped, be of service to many a young sailor in many a corner of the world.

CHAPTER 6

HOW TO MAKE
THE TOM THUMB
ICE-BOAT
AND LARGER
CRAFT

ALTHOUGH a full-rigged, delicately balanced ice-yacht looks like a very complicated piece of mechanism, when it is carefully examined the framework will be found to consist of two pieces crossing each other at right angles. The top of the cross is the bowsprit, the bottom of the cross the stern, and the sides the runners. At the intersection of the cross pieces the mast is stepped. The principle is simple enough, and with some sticks, two small pieces of inch lumber, three old skates, and two boards, a real little "Tom Thumb ice-yacht" can be built to hold a crew of one, and to be rigged like a catboat or with a jib and mainsail. The cross board may be made about 3 feet long and 6 inches wide. Make two runner blocks of inch lumber, and let them be each 6 inches long and 3 inches wide. With a bit and brace or a red-hot poker bore holes at proper distances apart for the straps of old-fashioned skates to pass through. One inch from each end of the cross board, fasten on the runner blocks securely with nails or screws (**FIG. 6-1**). For the centre plank use a board about 6 inches wide and 5 feet long. Nail the cross plank on to the centre plank in such

FIG. 6-1

End of Cross-board, showing Runner-block and Skate

FIG. 6-2

Rudder with Tiller-ropes

FIG. 6-3

Leg-of-mutton Sail

a manner that a line drawn through the centre of the latter will intersect the cross board exactly at its middle. The planks must be at right angles to each other, forming a cross, the centre piece extending about one foot beyond the cross piece; this end will be the bow of the ice-boat and the opposite end the stern. Bore a large hole in the stern for the rudder-post to pass through. The rudder-post may be made in a variety of forms; a simple and convenient one is shown by **FIG. 6-2**. Another hole must be made through the point where the centres of the cross and centre planks intersect for the mast. **FIG. 6-3** shows a leg-of-mutton sail, but the young yachtsman may make a sail of any description that may suit his taste. By referring back to the chapter on "How to Rig and Sail Small Boats," he can find several simple kinds of sails illustrated. **FIG. 6-4** shows the top view of an ice-boat a trifle larger than the one just described; the braces shown in the diagram are unnecessary on very small craft. To hold the mast more securely in larger yachts, a bench is made after the plan of **FIG. 6-5**; this will prevent the mast from being carried away under any ordinary circumstances, and also prevent it from swaying with every puff of wind. Where a seat is made as in **FIG. 6-4**, a wooden handle can be substituted for the tiller-ropes (**FIG. 6-6**).

The rudder is made of a skate; the latter is fastened by the screw at the heel and then strapped on a board nailed on to a club, shaped like a potato-

FIG. 6-4

Top View of Ice-Boat

masher; the small part of the club runs through a hole in the stern of the centre-board. A forked stick can be used for a tiller and must be fastened on to the rudder-post by running a pin or large wire through holes bored for the purpose in the rudder-post and the prongs of the forked stick. If the top of the rudder-post be squared, a tiller may be made of a stick with a square hole to fit over the end of the rudder-post, as shown in the illustration at the end of this chapter.

Mast Bench

Perhaps some of my readers will invent more ingenious and simple steering apparatus than the ones given here; if not, and the rudder-post and tiller seem to be a little too difficult, they may be omitted, and a stationary runner block substituted in their place. The boat must then be steered by the feet of the crew. To do this he should have on skates. If a long handle be attached to the stern like the back to a sleigh-chair, the steersman with skates on can guide the boat with his feet by standing behind and holding on to the handle at the stern. With this rig, the boat can accommodate a passenger aboard, as the steersman does not occupy the boat itself but tends the sheets and steers while being towed behind. A common sled may be fixed with holes in it so that a cross board can be attached by movable pegs, and with a mast stepped in the bow it will make tolerable speed and may be steered by a boy on skates.

Steering Apparatus

PART III
THE BOY FISHERMAN

CHAPTER 7

HOME-MADE FISHING TACKLE

The Rod

It not unfrequently happens that an amateur is unable to take advantage of most excellent fishing, for the want of proper or necessary tackle.

It may be that he is accidentally in the neighborhood of a pickerel pond or trout stream, or that his fishing tackle is lost or delayed in transit. Under such circumstances a little practical ingenuity is invaluable. If within reach of any human habitation you can, in all probability, succeed in finding sufficient material with which to manufacture not only a rod which will answer your purpose, but a very serviceable reel. To rig up a home-made trout rod, you need a straight, slender, elastic pole, such as can be found in any wood or thicket, some pins, and a small piece of wire. File off the head of several pins, sharpen the blunt ends, and bend them into the form of the letter U. At a point about two feet from the butt end of the rod drive the first pin, leaving enough of the loop above the wood

FIG. 7-1

FIG. 7-2

Construction of the Tin and Spool Reel

FIG. 7-3

to allow the fish line to pass freely through; drive the other pins upon the same side of the rod and at regular intervals. Make the tip of a piece of wire by bending a neat circular loop in the centre, and then knitting or binding the wire on the end of the pole (**FIG. 7-1**). Should you have enough wire, it will answer much better for the other loops than the pins. If at a farmhouse look in the attic for an old bonnet frame, or some similar object likely to be at hand, and it will furnish you with plenty of material. Cut the wire in pieces about two and a half inches long, make a simple loop in the centre of each piece, and with a "waxed end" or strong thread bind the ends of the wire lengthwise on the rod, then give each loop a turn, twisting it in proper position (**FIG. 7-2**). With a large wooden spool, an old tin can, and a piece of thick wire, a first-rate reel may be manufactured.

Tin and Spool Reel

FIG. 7-4

Put the wire through the spool, allowing about one inch to protrude at one end and about three inches at the opposite end. Wedge the wire in firmly by driving soft pine sticks around it, and trim off the protruding ends of the sticks. Cut a piece of tin in the shape shown by the diagram (**FIG. 7-3**), punch a hole in each side piece for the wire to pass through, leaving plenty of room for the spool to revolve freely. Turn the side-pieces up upon each side of the spool, and bend the long end of the wire in the form of a crank. Hammer the bottom piece of tin over the rod until it takes the curved form, and fits tightly, then with strong wax string bind it firmly to the rod. If it should happen that a piece of tin could not be procured, a reel can be made of a forked stick and a spool.

FIG. 7-5

The Forked-Stick Reel

Cut a forked stick and shave off the inside flat, as in **FIG. 7-4**, cut two notches near the bottom, one upon each side; this will allow the fork to bend readily at these points. Make a small groove for a string at the top of each prong. Put the spool between the prongs, allowing the wire to protrude through holes bored for that purpose. Bend the long end of the wire in the form of a crank. Tie a string across from end to end of the prongs to hold them in proper position, and you have a rustic but serviceable reel (**FIG. 7-5**). It may be attached to the pole in either manner shown by **FIGS. 7-6** and **7-7**. Boys who find pleasure in outdoor sports should always be ready with expedients for any emergency. A fish hook is rather a difficult thing to manufacture, though I have seen them made of a bird's claw bound to a piece of shell by vegetable fibre. I would not advise my readers to attempt to make one. A better plan is to always carry a supply about your person, inside the lining of your hat being a good place to deposit small hooks. For black bass, pickerel, and many other fish, live minnows are the best bait. To catch them you need a net.

FIG. 7-6

Home-Made Nets

A simple way to make a minnow net is to stretch a piece of mosquito netting between two stout sticks. If deemed necessary, floats may be fastened at the top and sinkers at the bottom edge of the net (**FIG. 7-8**). Coarse bagging may be used if mosquito netting is not obtainable. But with a forked

FIG. 7-7

FIG. 7-8

FIG. 7-9

stick and a ball of string for material, a jack-knife, and your fingers for tools, a splendid scoop-net can be made that will not only last, but be as good, if not better, than any you could purchase. Cut a good stout sapling that has two branches (**FIG. 7-9**). Trim off all other appendages, and bend the two branches until the ends over-lap each other for some distance, bind the ends firmly and neatly together with waxed twine, if it can be had—if not, with what string you have (**FIG. 7-10**).

Fasten the pole in a convenient position so that the hoop is about level with your face. If you want the net two feet deep, cut a number of pieces of twine seven or eight feet long, double them, and slip them on the hoop in the manner shown by the first string (**FIG. 7-11**).

Beginning at the most convenient point, take a

string from each adjoining pair and make a simple knot of them, as shown by the diagram. Continue all the way around the hoop knotting the strings together in this manner. Then commence on the next lower row and so on until you reach a point

FIG. 7-10

where, in your judgment the net ought to commence to narrow or taper down. This can be accomplished by knotting the strings a little closer together, and cutting off one string of a pair at four equidistant points in the same row. Knot as before until you come to a clipped line; here you must take a string from each side of the single one and knot them, being careful to make it come even with others in the same row. Before tightening the double knot pass the single string through, and after tying a knot close to the double one cut the string off close. (See **FIG. 7-11** A.)

Continue as before until the row is finished, only deviating from the original plan when a single string is reached. Proceed in a like manner with the next and the next rows, increasing the number of strings eliminated until the remaining ones meet at the bottom, being careful not to let one drop mesh come directly under another of the same kind.

A scoop-net can be made of a piece of mosquito netting by sewing it in the form of a bag, and fastening it to a pole and hoop made of a forked stick like the one just described. Minnows must be kept alive, and tin buckets, with the top half perforated with holes, are made for that purpose. These buckets,

FIG. 7-11

when in use, are secured by a string and hung in the water, the holes in the sides allowing a constant supply of fresh breathing material to the little fish within.

A Home-Made Minnow Bucket

Take any tin bucket that has a lid to it and punch holes in the top and upper part with a nail and hammer, or some similar instruments. If a tin bucket cannot be had, a large-sized tin can will answer the purpose. The illustration (**FIG. 7-12**) shows a minnow bucket made in this manner. **FIG. 7-13** shows the proper manner of baiting with a live minnow. The cartilaginous mouth of a fish has little or no feeling in it. A hook passed from beneath the under jaw through it and the upper lip will neither kill nor injure the minnow. As it allows the little creature to swim freely, there is a much greater chance of getting a bite than with a dead or mangled bait. The latter is a sign of either cruelty or ignorance on the part of the fisherman.

Inhabitants of the Water

How natural it is to speak of a love for the sea, or an intimate acquaintance and knowledge of the ocean, when, in reality, it is only the top or surface of the water that is meant, while the hidden mysteries that underlie the billows, the sea-world proper—its scenery, inhabitants, and history—are but partially known, except to our most learned naturalists. The occasional glimpses we have of queer and odd specimens kidnapped from this unknown realm make it natural for us to feel a curiosity to know and a desire to see the life and forms that are concealed beneath the waves.

What boy can sit all day in a boat, or upon the green shady bank of an inland stream, watching the floating cork of his fish line without experiencing a longing for some new patent transparent diving bell, in which, comfortably ensconced at the bottom of the water, he might see all that goes on in that unfamiliar country.

In Chapter 21 I propose to show how this natural curiosity or desire for knowledge may be gratified, not exactly by placing you at the bottom of the water, but by transporting a portion of this curious world, with its liquid atmosphere and living inhabitants into your own house, where you may inspect and study it at your leisure.

FIG. 7-13

CHAPTER 8

NOVEL MODES
OF FISHING

THE author, when a lad, was unable to learn to swim by following the directions in the books he had; nor did the articles on skating assist him in the least in learning to skate; but where a new game was described, or diagrams given for some boyish contrivance, such notes were of great assistance.

Now, I do not wish my readers to suppose that he will find an exhaustive discourse of fishing; what he will find is all the novelties in that line, with diagrams and explanations, that have come within the experience of the writer.

The Pistol Reporter

is a contrivance invented by a friend of the author, after he had experimented with the "Dancing Fisherman" described on page 95. The "Reporter's" float is made exactly in the same manner as the Dancing Fisherman's, but in the place of the jumping toy, an old-fashioned, single-barrelled pistol is securely lashed to the

FIG. 8-1

upright stick, and the fish-line tightly fastened to the trigger.

To prevent accidents my friend never loaded the pistol, but relied upon the noise of the exploding cap to notify him that there was something on the line. **FIG. 8-1** shows the Pistol Reporter. The common toy-pistol makes the best "Reporter," being smaller and more easily procured. One more invention, and the reader will have more than enough to occupy his time after the ordinary pole and line-fishing has grown tiresome.

The Floating Tip-Up

consists simply of a float, with a tip-up fastened at one end, as shown in **FIG. 8-2**. The flag-rod, being unevenly balanced, will fall upon the block, as is shown by one in the distance on the accompanying cut; but the slightest pull on the line will raise the flag, and warn the fisherman that there is something at the bait. **FIG. 8-2**, A, shows the simple manner in which the joint or hinge is made, by driving a long pin through the jaws of the upright and through the flag-pole, allowing about one-third of the pole to extend over the water for the attachment of the fish-line.

The Bell Pole

In the Gulf States, upon some of the plantations that border the sluggish streams or bayous peculiar to that part of the country, the field hands have a simple and ingenious contrivance by which they are enabled to fish without interfering with the discharge of their duties.

The apparatus used consists of an ordinary cane-pole to which a long line with any number of hooks is attached; an old bell is hung at the end of the cane where the line is fastened.

The sable sportsmen set a number of poles, rigged in this manner, thrusting the butt ends of the rods into the soft bank so that they stand almost upright along the edge of the water upon which the plantation borders.

After the hooks are baited the lines are cast out as far as they will reach into the stream and left to take care of themselves. As soon as a fish is hooked it struggles to free itself, but the first plunge the unwary creature makes rings the bell at the end of the rod and summons the laborer from the field, who leaves his ploughing or planting just long enough to land the fish and re-bait the hook. It is seldom that the setting sun sees the dusky workmen return to their cabins empty-handed.

By far the oddest and most original mode of fishing practised by the colored people of the Southern States is called by them

"Jugging for Cats"

Early one morning, while sauntering along the river at a small town upon the Mississippi, the author met an old colored friend, Uncle Eanes.

"Whars I gwine?" queried the old man. "I was jus gwine to git de traps together to jug for cats,—Hi, Hi, neber hea tell of dat? De Lor! no sah, not presactly pussy cats—cullored folks eats 'bout de same as white folks (when dey can git it). Yes, sah! we's seed purty tight times since de war, Suah! but we hasent come to eating pussy cats just yet, Boss! Hi, Hi! Take a big jug suah enough to hold a tolerable sized mud cat! but we don't cotch dem in de jugs. You jest come along and I'll show you how 'tis." Uncle Eanes's invitation was accepted, and the author was initiated into the mysteries of "jugging for cats," which he found to combine exercise, excitement and fun in a much greater degree than the usual method of angling with rod and reel.

The tackle necessary in this sport is very simple; it consists of five or six empty jugs tightly corked with corn cobs, as many stout lines, each about five feet long with a sinker and large hook at the end. One of these lines is tied to the handle of each jug. Fresh liver, angle worms,

FIG. 8-3

and balls made of corn meal and cotton, are used for bait; but a bit of cheese, tied up in a piece of mosquito netting to prevent its washing away, appears to be considered the most tempting morsel.

When all the hooks are baited, and the fisherman has inspected his lines and found everything ready, he puts the jugs into a boat and rows out upon the river, dropping the earthenware floats about ten feet apart in a line across the middle of the stream. The jugs will, of course, be carried down with the current, and will have to be followed and watched. When one of them begins to behave in a strange manner, turning upside down, bobbing about, darting up stream and down, the fisherman knows that a large fish is hooked, and an exciting chase ensues. It sometimes requires hard rowing to catch the jug, for often when the fisherman feels sure of his prize and stretches forth his hand to grasp the runaway, it darts off anew, frequently disappearing from view beneath the water, and coming to the surface again, yards and yards away from where it had left the disappointed sportsman.

One would think that the pursuit of just one jug, which a fish is piloting around, might prove exciting enough. But imagine the sport of seeing four or five of them start off on their antics at about the same moment. It is at such a time that the skill of a fisherman is tested, for a novice, in his hurry, is apt to lose his head, thereby losing his fish also. Instead of hauling in his line carefully and steadily, he generally pulls it up in such a hasty manner that the fish is able, by a vigorous flop, to tear himself away from the hook. To be a successful "jugger," one must be as careful and deliberate in taking out his fish as though he had only that one jug to attend to, no matter how many others may be claiming his attention by their frantic signals. The illustration shows how the line is rigged.

The Dancing Fisherman

is another method of catching fish, in principle similar to jugging, by means of a jumping-jack, or small, jointed man whose limbs are moved by jerking a string attached to them. This little figure is fastened to a stick, which is secured in an upright position on a float made of a piece of board. Through a hole in the float is passed the string attached to the figure, and tied securely to this are the hook and line. After the hook is baited, the float is placed on the surface of the water, and the little man, standing upright, is left to wait in patience.

Presently a fish, attracted by the bait, comes nearer the surface, seizes the hook quickly, and darts downward, pulling the string, and making the little figure throw up its arms and legs as though dancing for joy at having performed

FIG. 8-4

its task so well. The capering of Jack is the signal to his master that a fish has been caught and is struggling to free itself from the hook. This manner of fishing is necessarily confined to quiet bodies of water, such as small lakes or ponds; for in rough water poor little Jack would be upset. **FIG. 8-4** shows how to rig the "dancing fisherman."

Toy Boats for Fishing

Trolling, by means of rudely made toy boats, is a sport the novelty of which will certainly recommend itself.

The boat can be made out of a piece of plank any where from a foot to two and one-half feet long, according to the size of the fish to be caught. Sharpen the plank at one end and rig it with one or two masts and sails of paper or cloth. The rudder must be very long in proportion to the size of the boat, to prevent its making lee way and to keep it on a straight course. To nails in the stern of the boat tie fish lines rigged

FIG. 8-5

with spoon or live bait (**FIG. 8-5**). This diminutive fishing smack will not alarm the finny inhabitants of the water as a larger boat might, but when sailing before the wind will troll the bait in a manner that appears to be irresistible to bass or pickerel, and sometimes even the mud-loving cat-fish will rise and swallow the hook. A whole fleet of these little vessels may be attended by one boy if he has a boat in which to row immediately to the assistance of any of his toy boats, whose suspicious movements betray the presence of a fish in tow.

The Wooden Otter

consists of a board two feet long, three inches wide, and one-half-inch thick, made to float on edge in the water by weighting the lower part of the plank with lead, iron, or even stones, tied on with strings. By means of a breast-band rigged like that on a kite, a strong tow-line is fastened to the "otter." At intervals along the tow-line, shorter lines are attached baited with artificial flies, spoon hooks, dead or live bait, as the case may be, the bait of course depending altogether upon the fish you are after. As you walk or row, the "otter" sheers off and the baits comb the water in a tantalizing way that is fatal to trout, bass, or pickerel. So "killing" is this instrument that it should only be used to replenish the larder when provisions are running short in camp.

Fishing for Fresh-Water Clams

Mussels, or fresh-water clams, are prized by many boys on account of the pearly opalescent substance of which the shell is composed, it being an excellent material of which to make finger-rings and charms. Not unfrequently pearls of great beauty are found concealed within the shells of these bivalves.

The empty shells found upon the beach are never very highly prized, and are called by collectors dead shells. Shells of any kind which contain the living animal when collected, are ever after called live shells, for they still retain all their freshness and lustre after the inmate has been removed. To collect live mussel shells, you must wade, dive, or, if the water is clear enough for you to distinguish objects upon the bottom, fish for them, not with a hook and line, but with a long twig, from which all branches and leaves have been removed excepting a single bud on the end (**FIG. 8-6**). As soon as you detect a bivalve, you will discover its shells to be partially open.

Carefully insert the bud, that you have left upon the end of your stick, between the gaping lips of the shell, the instant that the animal within feels the touch it will close its doors firmly, of course holding the switch between the shells. The bud at the end prevents the stick from slipping out, and the animal is caught by taking advantage of the very means it uses for protection.

A simple contrivance for catching small frogs, eels, and lizards, for the aquarium consists of an elder stick, with one end cut like a quill pen with the points spread apart, as shown in sketch (**FIG. 8-7**).

To use this you must approach a pond or brook very cautiously so as not to frighten your game. Through the clear water the little creatures can be seen resting quietly on the bottom. If you are careful not to make any disturbance or sudden movement you may get your elder lance poised over your lizard, newt, or frog, within an inch or so of its body, without disturbing him; then with a quick movement push the stick and animal both into the mud. On drawing out the stick you will find your captive squirming between the split ends of the elder—from which he can be removed without serious injury. With practice you can perfect yourself in this aquarian sport so as seldom to lose or injure your specimens.

The snare made of fine wire in the form of a slip noose is so well known to the boys in general, that it is no novelty and unnecessary to describe.

FIG. 8-6

FIG. 8-7

CHAPTER 9

DREDGE TANGLE AND TRAWL FISHING

THIS new pastime not only insures the fisherman something to show for his day's work, but, by furnishing an incentive, it lends an additional charm to rowing or sailing, and combines the pleasures of fishing and boating, perhaps, in a greater degree than any other sport upon the list of out-door exercises. There is no good reason why the "dredge" and "tangle" should be monopolized by a few learned scientists, nor why the sport should not be indulged in by all boys, as well as men, who love the open air, the salt sea breeze, Nature and her wonders.

To put this new pastime within the reach of the boys, this chapter illustrates and describes the "regular" dredge made upon the most improved pattern, and it also shows how serviceable dredges and tangles may be made out of simple materials to be found about any house.

The dredge is an instrument made to drag along the bottom of the water and scoop up the objects, such as corals, sponges, etc, that are found there.

The common oyster dredge is a familiar object at all sea-side places, but it has two or three defects which make it objectionable to the amateur dredger. In the first place, it requires a skilled hand to keep it right side up when in use. Nothing is more discouraging to a beginner than to discover, after a long pull, that on account of the dredge being towed upside down the scraper has been unable to perform its

FIG. 9-1

FIG. 9-2

duty. The meshes of an oyster dredge are made very large purposely, that all small objects may slip through. Among these small objects are some of the curiosities most prized by the collector.

To remedy the first defect, the collector's dredge is made with a scraper upon both sides (**FIG. 9-1**). The second defect is overcome by using a net with very fine meshes.

The net, if unprotected, would soon be cut and torn into shreds by the sharp-edged shells or rough bottom. To prevent this, it is enclosed in a leather or canvas bag open at both ends (**FIG. 9-1**). The dotted line shows the net inside.

The handles and scrapers are composed of iron. If the machine become fast between the rocks of the bottom, the string that binds the joint marked in the diagram (**FIG. 9-1**) will part, thus allowing the machine to turn edgewise and free itself.

Many curious objects were frequently brought up clinging to the cable or the frayed edges of the canvas cover of the dredges first used, and it was noticed that the dredge itself seldom contained any of these objects. This fact gave birth to

The Tangle

a name given to tassels of hemp that are often attached to the bottom of the dredge itself or used separately (**FIGS. 9-2** and **9-3**).

The Trawl

If the bottom to be explored be smooth a trawl can be used (**FIG. 9-4**). This consists of a net larger than the one connected with the dredge. The front of the net is attached to a rod at the top and hangs slack at the bottom, being weighted by small sinkers. The rod is fastened to runners which allow the trawl to slide smoothly over the bottom. Weights are sometimes fastened to the ends of the runners. It is a good idea to have pockets in the net, to prevent the fish from escaping. The end of the net should be gathered and tied with a string, so that by untying the string the contents can be dumped out in less time than it takes to tell of it.

Old Chain Tangle

How to Make a Bake-Pan Dredge

There is a kind of flat sheet-iron pan used in the kitchen for holding bread or biscuit while baking. It is seldom that the cook cannot show you one of these pans (**FIG. 9-5**) that has served its time and been discarded. Such a one will make a first-rate frame for a dredge. The only difficulty will be found in cutting the bottom out neatly. If there be a tin shop in the neighborhood it is best to take the pan there and have the tinner cut it for you; or you may do it yourself with a can opener or some other convenient instrument. Cut as shown by the dotted lines in **FIG. 9-5**, which represents the pan bottom upwards. This will leave a margin of about an inch and a half still adhering to the pan; with a strong nail and a hammer punch holes all around the marginal piece of the bottom. Make two larger holes in each end to admit the ropes forming the handles.

Bend the bottom pieces out as illustrated by **FIG. 9-6**, and it will produce a compact and handy frame for a small dredge.

FIG. 9-5

The Trawl

An old coffee sack can be readily adapted so as to serve as a net, but if the canvas cover be used as in **FIG. 9-1**, mosquito netting of double thickness will answer for the inner pouch.

FIG. 9-7 shows a "bake-pan dredge" with ropes attached ready for use. Although the framework of a "regular" dredge can be made by any blacksmith at trifling cost, it is more fun to make a dredge for one's self. When once the principles upon which a machine is made are thoroughly understood, it requires but little ingenuity to produce home-made substitutes that will perhaps answer as well, if not better, than the originals.

A Tin-Pail Dredge

FIG. 9-6

Take any old tin bucket, knock the bottom out, and attach a piece of coffee sack for a net. Tie bunches of hemp to the rim, first punching holes for the purpose, and you will have a make-shift dredge like the one in the tail-piece that only requires a few minutes to manufacture. Even with such a crude apparatus as this, many things may be captured for the cabinet or aquarium, the hempen tangles serving not only to entangle star-fish, sea-urchins, and the like, but in a measure preventing other creatures their have been scooped up by the pail from making their escape.

How to Make a Broomstick Tangle

Saw off from an old broom handle a piece of stick about two and one-half feet long; hunt up three or four pieces of chain about the size used for large dog-chains; with small iron staples fasten these chains at intervals along the broomstick. Tie bunches of hemp securely along the chains. If you have no hemp, unravel pieces of old rope ends and tie them to the chains as in the illustration (**FIG. 9-2**). The broomstick, being light, will possibly float in spite of the chains. This can only be prevented by attaching weights to the stick.

If a couple of iron wheels can be procured and put upon the ends of the broomstick they will not only counteract the buoyancy of the stick, but will also, in a measure, prevent the tangle from fouling stones or other objects on the bottom.

In the place of the iron wheels, simple weights of lead or other material may be used, and instead of the chains, weighted strings can be tied to the stick and the hempen knots fastened to them. Still another tangle can be made of a piece of old chain.

Bake-Pan Dredge

The Old Chain Tangle

as may be seen by the illustration (**FIG. 9-3**), is simply a piece of iron chain decorated with hempen tassels and occasional cross-sticks. A rope is attached to one end, and by its means the tangle is hauled over the bottom to gather up its load of curiosities.

Hints and Suggestions to Amateurs

If dredging from a sail-boat, divide the crew into two parties, one to manage and sail the boat, the other to attend to the casting and hauling of the dredge. It is as necessary that the boat be carefully managed as it is that at least one person's un-divided attention be given to handling the dredge. The dredging rope should be about twice as long as the water is deep. A wooden reel or windlass attached to one side of the boat near the stern will be of very great assistance, especially when the net comes up filled with mud or heavy stones, as it frequently does; in which case, if there be but one boy to attend to it he will find it no light task to pull in the line hand over hand.

FIG. 9-8

A piece of old oilcloth or tarpaulin will answer to dump the contents of the dredge upon, although a large wooden tray, or "picking-over board," as it is called, is much better. A small board of the kind intended for a row-boat is shown in the illustration at the head of this chapter.

Common glass preserve jars, or wide-mouthed bottles, make excellent receptacles for living specimens. A convenient rack for carrying these easily and safely may be made from any wooden box, by nailing laths or slats across the top from end to end and side to side, making the squares thus formed just large enough to hold the jars or bottles in an upright position.

The sail-boat is best for long excursions, but for a short trip a row-boat is preferable, it being more readily handled and independent of the wind.

Although a dredge without tangles will bring up many curious and interesting objects, the specimens are apt to be confined to the mollusca or shell-fish, mixed, of course, with all manner of rubbish.

If properly managed, the pouch, when it reaches the surface, will be about half full. After it has been emptied upon the "picking-over" board, the mud and sand may be washed away by pouring water over the mass. Although not absolutely necessary, a large sieve is a desirable addition to the dredger's outfit, and furnishes valuable assistance when the mud or sand is to be searched for minute objects. Some dredgers use a "nest of sieves," so arranged that the strainers, four in number, fit freely within one another. The top sieve is of course smaller than the others, but the meshes are larger. The second sieve is a little larger, with finer meshes. The third is still larger, with a much finer mesh, and the fourth, the largest sieve of the lot, has a mesh so close as only to allow the finest sand or mud to pass through. The contents of a dredge when filtered through a "nest of sieves" is divided up into a graduated series, the largest objects at the top and the smallest at the bottom. Mr. Emerton, in his "Life on the Seashore," describes a sieve for hanging over the side of a boat "in the shape of a half cylinder," the bottom being made of strong wire; but, as before remarked, sieves are not absolutely necessary, and may be dispensed with when the object is only a day's fun with the curiosities of the sea.

The Use of the Tangle

Partially buried in the mud of the bottom are to be found many pretty corals, queer and curious sponges, and those funny animals called sea-cucumbers. The dredge may skip these, but the hempen tangles, when they sweep the bottom, catch all such rough or irregular objects and bring them to the surface, along with a miscellaneous assortment of star-fish, sea-urchins, crabs, shrimps, and hundreds of other creatures.

Wyville Thomson, in his interesting account of the dredging cruise of the Porcupine and Lightning, mentions one haul when the tangles contained not fewer than 20,000 sea-urchins, which "were warped through and through the hempen fibres and actually filled the tangles; and," adds Mr. Thomson, "they hung for days round the bulwarks like nets of pickling onions in a green-grocer's shop." At times the tangle, when it comes to the surface, is completely covered with curious little shrimplike creatures called Caprellas. Indeed, so many surprises await the dredger and tend to keep up the excitement, that this new sport cannot fail to interest and delight all who participate in it; and when the young dredgers return home they need not do so empty-handed, but may, if they choose, bring curiosities from the bottom of the sea that will not only astonish their parents, but most likely puzzle their teachers and professors.

CHAPTER 10

WINTER FISHING

THE pleasures of fishing are naturally and almost invariably connected in our minds with warm weather, particularly with Spring or the first coming of Summer, the bright freshness of bursting bud and new-opening wild blossom, and with those latter days in the Autumn over which the Summer King sheds his brightest glories. But in our northern and easterly States, when old Winter has spread his mantle of frost and snow over the face of Nature, and hermetically sealed all the lakes and ponds under covers of ice, as an agreeable addition to the fun of skating, hardy, red-cheeked boys cut round holes in the thick ice, and through them rig their lines for pickered fishing. A very simple but ingenious contrivance enables a single fisherman to attend to quite a number of lines if the holes be all made within sight of the fisherman, the fish itself will give the signal for the particular line that requires attention.

FIG. 10-1

The construction of this automatic fishing-tackle is so simple that it may be made in a few moments by any one. The preceding illustration shows how it is arranged (**FIG. 10-1**). At the end of a light rod a foot or two in length is fastened a small signal flag; a piece of any bright-colored cloth answers the purpose. This rod is bound with strong string at right angles to a second stick, which is placed across the hole, lying some inches upon the ice at either side; the flag also rests on the ice, leaving a short piece of the flag-rod projecting over the cross stick; to this short end the line and hook are fastened. The hook is baited with a live minnow or other suitable bait and lowered through the hole. The tackle is then in readiness for the capture of a pickerel. When the fish is hooked his struggles keep the flag flying (**FIG. 10-2**).

The Signal Flying

Smelt Fishing
and the Smelt Fisher's House

From about December 20th until the middle or latter part of February the smelt fishing season is in its height along the coast of Maine. The fish are caught through holes in the ice. In the vicinity of Belfast clam worms are used for bait; the worms are found in the clam flats.

Notwithstanding the reputation for original inventions possessed by the inhabitants of the Eastern States, the "Down East" smelt fishermen of Maine have for years, while fishing through the ice, exposed themselves to the piercing winter winds, apparently without once thinking of providing any other shelter than their heavy overcoats and perhaps a rude barricade of ice blocks and evergreen boughs. There is no telling how long this state of things might have continued, but during the winter of 1877-78[*] a single fisherman, more enterprising than his comrades, appeared upon the fishing grounds with a small canvas tent, inside of which he at once proceeded to make himself comfortable, and at the same time excite the envy of the unprotected, shivering fishermen scattered over

---

[*] According to the Belfast (Mc.) Journal.

the ice. The latter were not long in taking the hint, and the next season found the ice dotted all over with the little canvas houses of the fishermen. During the best of the season the smelt fishing grounds now have the appearance of Indian villages; the blue smoke curls up from the peaked roofed lodges and floats away on the frosty air, while the figures of men and boys passing to and fro on different errands might at a distance be easily mistaken for the aboriginal red Americans at their winter camp.

The framework of a smelt fisher's house consists of a light wooden frame about six feet square, with a sharp roof. After the frame is firmly fastened together it is put upon runners, furnished with a bench for the fisherman to sit upon, a stove to keep him warm, and a covering of light canvas to keep out the cold. The canvas is a better protection against sleet and frost if it has been covered with a coat of paint. Sometimes the houses are made large enough to accommodate more than one fisherman. Snugly ensconced beside a warm stove, with pipe in mouth, the old veterans spin their yarns, and, oblivious to the raging northwest winds, watch their lines, which are attached to a rack overhead and hang down, passing through a hole in the ice. The bait dangles about eight or ten feet under the water. When a fish bites, the motion of the line apprizes the fisherman of the fact, and he pulls it out, unhooks the fish and again drops his line. In this manner one man will succeed in catching from ten to fifteen pounds in a day.

A gentleman who seems to be posted upon the subject of smelt fishing sends me the following device, which ought to have been included in the chapter on odd modes of fishing. My correspondent says: "During the fall months the smelt run in large schools up the creeks and streams emptying into the ocean, and are caught with seines or nets by professional fishermen for market. To be sure, no true sportsman could make use of such means for capturing game; still, as it is necessary to take these small fish in large numbers to make a respectable mess, some ingenious sportsman has evolved a fishing-tackle with which one can legitimately do wholesale fishing. To a line on an ordinary pole is attached an apparatus resembling an umbrella-frame without

FIG. 10-3

The Umbrella Smelt Tackle

the handle; from the point of each bow hangs a line and hook (**FIG. 10-3**); in this way six or eight smelt may be taken in the time it would require to catch one with a single line."

For boys who live inland where smelt fishing is out of the question, there are other fish whose gamy nature will impart more fun and excitement to their capture. Long rods would be out of place within the narrow limits of a little cloth-covered fishing box; but hand lines or short rod and reel may be used. When a short rod is used it is only for the purpose of facilitating the use of the reel, and the rod should not be over two and one-half feet long. Fish may also be snared or speared through holes in the ice by boys concealed in little wooden shanties built for the purpose. This sport is much in vogue on some of the small lakes in the Northwest.

The Spearsman's Shanty

The great drawback to spearing fish through holes in the ice, is the inability of the spearsman to see objects under water, and to keep the cold winds from chilling him through and through as he stands almost motionless watching for his game; but if the sportsman will supply himself with one of the little wooden shanties used by the fish spearers in the Northwest, he will overcome both these difficulties. The shanty, when the door is closed, is perfectly dark inside, having no other opening except a round hole, about a foot and a half in diameter, in the floor just over the hole in the ice. The only light seen by the fisherman is the bright, shining water, which glows like a full moon underneath him. As his eyes become accustomed to the peculiar condition of things, the nebulous objects first discernible in the luminous water resolve themselves into floating grasses and reeds; the bottom, even where the water is quite deep, becomes plainly visible, and every passing fish is distinctly seen by the spearsman, while he, being in total darkness, is invisible to the creatures below. This effect can be readily understood when one remembers that the ice, unless it be covered with snow, is transparent, and that the light shining through illuminates the water. It is as if you were standing outside of a house on a very dark night looking through a window into a brilliantly lighted room.

The fishermen's shanties are provided with small sheet-iron stoves, which require but very little fire to make the house warm enough for one to sit with his coat off. The stoves are provided with small pipes, which issue through the roof or side of the house. A bench, camp-stool, or chair complete the furniture.

Snaring Fish

Catfish may be chummed for; that is attracted by bait cut up and dropped through the hole in the ice. The bait will attract many other fish, which can be snared with a slip-noose made of fine copper or brass wire and attached to the end of a line. There is nothing alarming in the looks of this instrument, and a fish will not notice the snare until it finds the fatal noose lightly drawn about its body. It requires a little practice to snare fish successfully. I well remember my first attempt. A large "mud sucker" was discovered under an overhanging bank. Cautiously I crept to the edge of the stream, and with trembling, yet careful hand, I let the snare glide gently into the water. The fish did not move; by degrees I slipped the noose over the comical slippery head of the creature, and with a mighty jerk landed—not the fish, but my snare in the boughs of a tree that overhung the water. I was thunderstruck when I discovered that the fine wire of the snare had cut the fish completely in halves, and as the muddy water, stirred up by the commotion beneath, rolled away down stream, I beheld one-half of the "mud sucker" with the puckering mouth still moving, and the other half with its tail flapping in the water beneath.

It requires experience to learn just how hard to pull on a snare to catch a fish and hold it without breaking the line or cutting the game.

FIG. 10-4

Framework for Spearman's Shanty

Spearing Fish

is far more exciting and sportsmanlike than snaring them. The fish may be attracted by dead bait dropped through the hole in the ice, after the manner before described, or if it be pickerel you are after, a trolling spoon can be danced up and down, and round and round, until it attracts the attention of the fish. Some fishermen use a wooden minnow weighted at the bottom with lead and provided with fins and tail made of tin. Such a decoy, to be effective, should be decorated with a brilliant red stripe on each side, a white belly, and a bright green back. By means of a line fastened to the wooden fish it can be made to swim around under water in a most frisky and life-like manner, completely deceiving the unwary pickerel. The decoy must be kept out of reach when the fish dart at it, and at the same time the spear must be poised, ready to cast at the first opportunity. Often the unsuspicious pickerel will stop and remain for some moments motionless directly under the hole in the ice, apparently considering the best mode of capturing the lively and gaudy minnow that dances so temptingly near his hungry jaws. This is a golden opportunity for the young fisherman, and waiting only such time as it may require to take aim, the lance should be launched. A good fish spear is described on page 121 and illustrated by **FIG. 11-4**. As soon as a fish is speared it should be thrown upon the ice outside the shanty and allowed to freeze. In this manner the meat is kept much sweeter and fresher than it is possible to preserve fish in warm weather, even for so short a time as it requires to carry the game home from the fishing grounds.

How to Build a Fishing House

FIG. 10-4 shows the framework for a small fishing house; the posts and cross pieces are made of such sticks as can be found along the bank of any stream or lake. **FIG. 10-5** shows how the floor is made of planks, with a hole in the forward part to fish through. The

FIG. 10-5

Floor and Runners of Spearman's Shanty

whole frame may be covered with pieces of an old hay-cover, canvas, or what is better still, pieces of old oil cloth, such as is used for dining-room or hall floors. If the framework be covered with any light cloth, the cloth should be tacked on and thickly coated with paint so as to admit no light. A frame like the one illustrated by **FIGS. 10-4** and **10-5** may be made, fitted up, and kept stored away until wanted for use. After hauling it out on the fishing grounds and cutting a hole through the ice, the frame can be covered with thick blankets, and without injuring the material the covering can be fastened by pins and strings over the framework and removed when the day's sport is finished. If, instead of rough forked sticks, regular square posts be used, the whole can be covered with quarter-inch pine lumber, thus making a light but serviceable shanty. If the light come in under the house, pack snow around it. If the snow cover the ice to such a thickness as to darken the water beneath, sweep a place clean around your shanty, and the light admitted through the clear ice will illuminate the water beneath your hut or tent. **FIG. 10-6** shows another form of fisherman's hut, made upon the same principle as the cabin of the Crusoe raft (**FIGS. 4-3** and **4-4**, page 34). Select hickory

FIG. 10-6

Crusoe Cabin Style

or any other elastic saplings, taking care to have them all about the same size. After boring holes with an auger in the side bars of the floor frame, bend saplings over and force their ends into the holes as shown in the diagram. The floor can be laid in the same manner as illustrated by **FIG. 10-5**, and the whole frame covered with some opaque fabric, or cloth made opaque by a coating of paint. A very beautiful and light fishing house might be made with a bamboo frame that could be taken apart and packed away for the summer like a jointed fishing-rod.

PART IV
THE BOY HUNTER

CHAPTER 11

HOME-MADE HUNTING APPARATUS, ETC.

can remember the boys with whom I used to play who were wonderful marksmen with stones, using only their arm and hand to propel them.

In Virginia there is said to live a young man, named Cross, who goes hunting without a gun, his sole and only weapons being smooth round stones, which he carries in his pockets. Throwing stones, he kills not only hares but partridges. Three respectable and truth-telling men assured the correspondent of the Richmond Telegram that they went out one day with him, they taking their guns; that he killed that day, using nothing but stones thrown from his hand, six hares running, and three partridges flying. He attended the State Fair, where a showman exhibited rag-babies arranged on steps, and charged five cents for two throws with a ball, at say ten paces. If you struck a baby, he gave you a prize and charged nothing. You have doubtless seen the game. Cross went in, threw and struck, and struck and threw, knocking over a baby at every pop until he broke up the show.

If such skill can be acquired with the unassisted hand and arm the reader may readily see that there are still greater possibilities with many of the home-made weapons described in this book.

Archery

There are innumerable books written on this sport, and consequently it does not fall under the list of subjects appropriate to the American Boy's Handy Book, except in the form of an introduction to some homemade weapons.

Archery as a fashionable recreation is now upon the ebb, but archery for boys is, and has been always, a popular an inexpensive pastime.

The bold Robin Hood is still the boy's hero. He was an outlaw, but outlaws in his days were often more respectable than the polished courtiers who followed the king. Robin Hood's fame, as a bowman, has done not a little to add to the popularity of the sport, although the best authorities of to-day claim that the tales of the wonderful feats in archery by this bold outlaw and his men cannot be regarded as strictly true. A writer for the New York *Sun* says that: "The longest distance that an arrow has been sent from a bow, the record of which may be regarded as authentic, is 972 yards. This tremendous feat was accomplished by Selim, grand Seignor of Turkey, in 1798. The record was carefully taken by Sir Robert Ainslie, at that time British representative at the Turkish court. The bows of to-day could not throw an arrow under the best conditions half that distance. The Turks made their bows to use as weapons, and they were accordingly long and heavy, and the arrow that Selim shot was a light one. One of the best long records made in England was the work of a Turkish bow and a Turkish archer. It was in 1792, when Mahmoud Effendi, secretary to the Turkish Embassy, shot an arrow a distance of 482 yards. The best bows of the present time find their limit at about 400 yards. These records are simply indicative of the strength of the bows and the archers."

FIG. 11-1

The Buckeye Bow

Occasionally we hear of some good work with a bow in our own country. Not long since, when a flock of wild geese passed over Virginia

City and wheeled in one of their circles, Otey, the long-bowman and "Lone Archer of the Sierra," sent a shaft among them. It was a long shaft, but it was well aimed. It went whizzing through the air and penetrated one of the wings of a flyer, causing it to flutter and lose place in the flock, which proves that we have some experts in this country who do not belong to the red-skinned fellows, who are being so rapidly and shamefully exterminated in the West.

My readers, I hope, are perfectly able to make their own weapons, and need not call upon their parents for money to buy shop-made outfits, for they are expensive. The best yew bows for ladies cost from $18 to $50 each; the same for gentlemen, $20 to $100 each. Arrows for ladies are for $3.50 to $11 per dozen; for gentlemen $5 to $12 per dozen. Practising arrows can be bought as low as $1.50 to $5.00 per dozen. Bowstrings cost 25 to 50 cents each. For ladies, quivers cost $1.50 to $2.75 each; for gentlemen $2.50 to $3.50 each. The rest of the outfit consists of arm-guards, $1 to $2 each; shooting gloves, 75 cents to $2 each; tips for bows, 50 to 75 cents per pair, and tassels, 50 to 75 cents each. Targets can be bought all the way from $1 to $7 apiece; target-stands, $2.50 to $5 each; green baize bow-covers, 75 cents each, and scoring-cards and tablets, ivory and ebony prickers, 25 cents to $2 apiece.

American boys love novelties and improvements on all things; and if we cannot improve on Robin Hood's long bow, we can at least introduce

The Buckeye Bow,

which to most boys will be a novelty, and does away with the constant liability to lose your arrows (**FIG. 11-9**).

The illustrations here given show a new sort of bow, and a manner of using it that avoids the above difficulty.

Split a good strong barrel-stave, and whittle it into the form of a bow, two inches wide at the centre, and tapering to about three-quarters of an inch at each end. It is necessary to strengthen with another piece

FIG. 11-2

of stave, spliced on to the centre. Let the splice be one-third the length of the bow. Through the centre of the bow and splice, bore a hole large enough for the arrow to fit it loosely (**FIG. 11-2**).

Make the arrow of any tough, straight-grained wood, in the form shown by **FIG. 11-3**. Let it be at least three-quarters of an inch thick at the thick end. Use great care to make the thick end terminate at right angles, or, to use a boy's term, "squarely," at a distance from the notch exactly equal to the distance from the middle of the string to the centre of the bow when it is strung (see **FIG. 11-3**).

Fill your ammunition bag with buckeyes, horse-chestnuts, or small potatoes. Clay and putty may be manufactured into balls and used as missiles.

This will make an outfit which will serve to amuse any boy, and, as with all other weapons, by practice great skill may be acquired in its use.

Spearing Fish

FIG. 11-3

"I don't know! Shure I *niver tried*," is the answer reported to have been made by an Irishman, when asked if he could play the fiddle. No doubt there are many boys who would give a like reply if asked if they could spear a fish.

An amateur's first attempt at casting a spear will probably meet with about the same success as "Paddy" might be expected to achieve in his first trial of a fiddle; but almost anything can be accomplished by practice. The keen enjoyment of the fisher who by his skill and dexterity has succeeded in striking a fine fish, can only be compared to the pleasant triumph of his brother sportsman in the field who has just secured two birds by a difficult double-shot.

How to Make a Fish Spear

Make the shaft or handle of any straight stick or pole seven or eight feet long; trim it down, and test the weight occasionally by balancing it in the hand. When the shaft seems to be about the proper weight, it should be let alone, and attention directed to the barbs for the head of the spear.

In place of the ordinary single point generally used as a spear head, the fishing spear may be supplied with two points, as shown in the illustration (**FIG. 11-4**). Any hard, elastic material will do for the head, split bamboo or cane, two pieces of heavy iron wire, filed to a point and notched into barbs upon the inside, as shown in the diagram, or the points may be made of bone like the fish arrows used by the inhabitants of Vancouver's Island. Very hard wood will also answer for the spear head. After the head pieces are notched and pointed, they should be firmly bound to the spear at a point a few inches below the end of the shaft. A couple of small wedges driven in between the shaft and the points will diverge the latter, as in the illustration. After this is accomplished, lash the barbs firmly on up to the head of the shaft. If a fish be struck by one of these weapons, it will be next to impossible for it to escape. The elastic points at first suddenly spread apart as the spear strikes the fish's body; the next instant they violently contract, holding the fish a secure prisoner. The barbs upon the inside prevent the prey from slipping out, no matter how smooth and slimy his body may be.

A small instrument made upon a similar plan can be used for catching snakes or other reptiles that are not safe or pleasant to handle. Frogs may also be readily captured with a fish spear, and any boy who takes the time to make one of these weapons will find himself amply

FIG. 11-4

Fish Spear and Enlarged View of Spear Head

repaid for his trouble. The elder stick described and illustrated upon page 97 is made upon the same principle as the fish spear.

Armed with fish spears and torches great fun can be had spearing fish from a row-boat at night. The torch illuminates the water and appears to dazzle the fish, at the same time disclosing their whereabouts to the occupants of the boat, who with poised spears await a favorable opportunity to strike the scaly game.

How to Make the Torches and Jack-Lights

One way to make a torch is to wind lamp-wick upon a forked stick (**FIG. 11-5**). The ball of wick must be thoroughly saturated with burning fluid of some kind. The torches should all be prepared before starting upon the excursion.

Never take a supply of kerosene or any explosive oil with you in the boat, for, in the excitement of the sport, accidents of the most serious nature may happen. A safe light can be made with a number of candles set in a box. A glass front allows the light to shine through, and a piece of bright tin for a reflector behind adds brilliancy to the illumination. A box of this description is generally called a "jack-box;" it is much less trouble than the flaring pine-knot or wick-ball torches.

The candles in the "jack-box" should be replenished each time after it is used; in this manner the jack may be kept always ready for use. After the candles are lighted fasten the box in the bow of the boat; here it will throw a bright light ahead, illuminating the water, but casting a heavy, dark shadow in the boat, concealing the occupants from view. The boys in the boat can, of course, see all the better for being themselves in shadow.

FIG. 11-5

Wick-torch

Whittling

Some have been trying to claim for the practice of whittling an English origin, and in a little work, published in London in 1774, entitled "The

Sentimental Exhibition; or, Portraits and Sketches of the Times," may be found the following statement: "M. Grosse, or some other Frenchman, remarks, that when we English have no other employment, we are sure to do mischief, and, therefore, when a parcel of sailors go into an inn at Wapping,

FIG. 11-6

*Elastic Gun—
The Stock*

the landlord delivers to each of them a stick and a knife with which to amuse himself, that they may not be destroyed the host's furniture."

In Kentucky and all through the Southwest, fifty years ago, it was the custom to have piled up on the hotel counter a lot of neat cedar sticks. Each guest, as he left the dining-room, selected a stick, and, taking out his jack-knife, commenced to whittle as he talked. So universal was the habit that he probably would have been unable to talk without whittling. The author has seen the most complicated wooden chairs and cubes, with moveable balls inside, that were whittled out of solid sticks by some of these old-time experts, and are now kept as curiosities by their children.

Now, however, whittling is confined mostly to boys, and, as the Americans are noted for their practical ideas, there is no reason why American boys should not make something of use, at least to themselves, with their jack-knives. Suppose my reader commences with a piece of straight-grained pine, about one or one-and-a-half inch thick, and free from knots.

The Elastic Gun

Carved a gun-stock in the form of **FIG. 11-6**, smoothe it nicely, and cut a slot (A) for the trigger.

The Sling

Cut a piece of wood long enough to project about one inch or more on each side of the barrel (B, **FIG. 11-7**), and screw it firmly to the muzzle. Near the ends of the cross-piece, put screw-eyes, and attach a strong

FIG. 11-7

FIG. 11-8

elastic to each screw-eye (C, C, **FIG. 11-7**). To the elastics fasten a soft leather sling with strong cords. A still more simple way is to screw the screw-eyes one on each side of the muzzle of the gun, and fasten the elastics on to them.

The Trigger

Make the trigger of a piece of perfectly straight hoop-iron, three or four inches long; with a nail, punch two holes in it; bend about half an inch of one end of the iron at right angles; then make a triangular block of wood, and bore a hole in one corner, and with a screw fasten the hoop-iron on securely; fasten one end of a short string to the hole in the straight end of the hoop-iron, and to the other end of the strings attach a ring.

Put the trigger in the slot (A, **FIG. 11-6**), and let it fit closely but move freely. Put a screw into the stock so that it will run through the corner of the triangle of the trigger and through the stock to hold the trigger in place.

Slip a strong rubber band along the trigger (E, **FIG. 11-9**), and the gun is finished and ready to use.

The boy who invented this gun as an improvement on the one described on page 130, states that it will shoot with great accuracy and force. After a little practice he claims that he could snuff a candle at fifty feet.

The Boomerang

We might expect strange weapons to come from a land that produces quadrupeds with heads like ducks, and other great beasts that go bounding over the plains like some immense species of jumping spiders, using their thick tails as a sort of spring to help them in leaping, and carrying their young in their fur-lined vest pockets! Nor will we be disappointed when, after viewing the duckbill and the kangaroo, we see the odd-looking clubs called boomerangs, or the simple but ingenious throw-sticks by means of which the native Australians are enabled to cast their weapon, with the greatest accuracy, an astonishingly long distance.

FIG. 11-9

The boomerang, or bommer-ang as it is sometimes called, is one of the most mysterious weapons known. Evolved by slow degrees from a simple war club by the ignorant and savage Australians, this instrument excites the interest and astonishes the civilized man by its strange and apparently unaccountable properties. To all appearances it is a simple, roughly hewn club, yet its movements when thrown by an expert hand are so eccentric as to make it a curious anomaly even to persons educated in natural philosophy. Whatever is wonderful or marvellous is always a subject of peculiar interest to mankind generally, but to boys an inexplicable natural phenomenon is a treasure-trove of immeasurable value.

How to Make a Boomerang

With boiling water scald a piece of well-seasoned elm, ash, or hickory plank that is free from knots. Allow the wood to remain in the water until it becomes pliable enough to bend into the form indicated by **FIG. 11-10**. When it has assumed the proper curve, nail on the side pieces A, A (**FIG. 11-10**) to hold the wood in position until it is thoroughly dry; after which the side pieces may be removed, with no fear that the plank will not retain the curve imparted.

FIG. 11-10

Saw the wood into as many pieces as it will allow (**FIG. 11-11** B), and each piece will be a boomerang in the rough that only needs to be trimmed up with a pocket-knife, and scraped smooth with a piece of broken glass to make it a finished weapon.

FIG. 11-11

FIG. 11-12

Miniature Boomerang

A large wood-rasp or file is of great assistance in shaping the implement. **FIG. 11-11** C shows a finished boomerang. **FIG. 11-11** D shows a cross section of the same. The curve in no two boomerangs is exactly the same; some come round with a graceful sweep, while others bend so suddenly in the middle that they have more the appearance of angles than curves. Just what the quality is that makes a good boomerang is hard to discover, although, as a rule, the one that appears to have the best balance and feels as if it might be thrown easily is the best.

To Throw a Boomerang

grasp the weapon near one end and hold it as you would a club; be careful to have the concave side, or hollow curvature, turned from you and the convex side toward you. Take aim at a stone, tuft of grass or other object on the ground about a hundred yards in front of you, and throw the weapon at the object. The weapon will in all probability not go anywhere near the mark, but, soaring aloft, perform some of the most extraordinary manœuvres, then starting off again with apparently renewed velocity, either return to the spot from where it was thrown or go sailing off over the fields like a thing possessed of life. A boomerang cast by a beginner is very dangerous in a crowd, for there is no telling where it is going to alight, and when it does come down it sometimes comes with force enough to cut a small dog almost in two.* Select a large open field where the ground is soft and there is no one around to be hurt. In such a field you may amuse yourself by the day throwing these curious weapons, and you can in this manner learn how to make the boomerang go through all manner of the most indescribable movements seemingly at your bidding.

---

* "I have seen a dog killed on the spot, its body being nearly cut in two by the boomerang as it fell."—Rev. J. G. Wood.

The Miniature Boomerang

here represented is supposed to be cut out of a card. The shape given in the illustration is a very good one, but it may be varied to an almost unlimited degree. Card boomerangs over an inch or so in length do not work well, but they may be made very much smaller.

One of these tiny instruments cannot be grasped by the hand, but when it is to be launched upon its eccentric journey the toy should be laid flat upon a card, allowing one end to project from the side as in **FIG. 11-12**. Take hold of the lower left hand corner of the card with the left hand, and with the forefinger of the right hand fillip the boomerang, striking it a quick, smart blow with the finger-nail, and the little missile will sail away, going through almost the same manœuvres that the large wooden boomerang does when thrown from the hand. Small boomerangs can be whittled out of a shingle with a pocket knife, and considerable amusement had with them; these small affairs can be thrown on the crowded playground, where it would be exceedingly dangerous to experiment with the larger and heavier club before described.

The Whip-Bow

This graceful and powerful weapon is like an ordinary longbow, with the exception that the bow-string is made fast to but one end, after the manner of a whip-lash; where the whip-lash terminates in a "snapper," the bow-string ends in a hard, round knot (**FIG. 11-13**); the arrow is made like any other arrow, either with a blunt end or a pointed spear-point. In one side of the arrow a notch is cut (**FIG. 11-14**, A); the bow-string being slipped into this notch, the knot at the end of the string prevents the arrow from slipping off until thrown by the archer, who, taking the butt of the whip-bow in his right hand, holds the arrow at the notch with his left hand, as in the illustration; then swaying

FIG. 11-13

Position Assumed when Casting the Arrow

FIG. 11-14

Whip Bow

FIG. 11-15

Using the Throw-
Stick

his body from side to side, he suddenly lets go with his left hand, at the same time extending his right arm to its full length from his side; this not only gives the arrow all the velocity it would acquire from the bow, but adds the additional force of a sling, thus sending the projectile a greater distance. The only place that I have seen the whip-bow used is on the lake shore in Northern Ohio. In some parts of this section it used to be a great favorite among the boys, who would throw the arrows up perpendicularly an amazing distance. Arrows can be bought in any city, but most boys prefer to make their own, leaving the "store arrows" for the girls to use with their pretty "store bows." The essential quality in an arrow is straightness. A spear-head can be made of an old piece of hoop-iron, a broken blade of a knife, or any similar piece of iron or steel, by grinding it down to the proper form and then binding it on to the shaft with fish line, silk, or a "waxed end," such as shoemakers use, or the arrow may have a blunt end with a sharp-pointed nail in the head. These arrows should only be used in target practice or when after game; they are dangerous on the play-ground. A simple whip-bow may be made by any boy in a few minutes out of an elastic sapling or branch, and an arrow cut out of a pine shingle with a pocket-knife. This can be improved upon as much as may be desired by substituting a piece of straight-grained, well-seasoned wood for the green branch, and regularly made Indian arrows for the crude pine ones.

Throw-Sticks

The same race that invented the wonderful boomerang also originated the equally ingenious throw-stick illustrated by **FIG. 11-16**. Although any of my readers can, in a few moments, fashion a throw-stick from a piece of wood by the aid of a pocket-knife, I doubt if they could use the instrument to any advantage without considerable practice.

FIG. 11-16

Throw-Sticks

Make the lance of cane or bamboo; use a straight piece and put an arrow-head upon one end; then holding the lance on a throw-stick, as shown by the accompanying illustration, cast it with all your might. The first trials will, doubtless, be failures, but nothing is gained without practice; and when you once "catch the hang of the thing" you will be astonished to see what a distance a comparatively small boy can throw a spear. Any straight, thin stick may be used as a lance. Allow one end to rest against the point upon the throw-stick, which will hold it in place until the cast is made. The throw-stick acts as a sling, lending additional force to the arm, and sending the spear much further than the strongest man can cast it with his unaided hand.

The Bird-Bolas

Probably all of my readers have read of that wonderful sling called a "bolas," used by some tribes of savages for the capture of game, but I doubt if any of them ever tried to manufacture one for themselves. Yet this curious missile can be made by a boy, and if he be inclined to field sports, he will find that a bird-bolas will do considerable execution.

FIG. 11-17

Bird-Bolas

Hunt for a half dozen round stones about the size of large marbles, or, better still, take six leaden musket-balls, wrap each ball in a piece of an old kid glove, buckskin, or cloth, as shown by the diagram (a, b, **FIG. 11-17**). Take three pieces of string each five feet long, double them in the centre, and bind the doubled parts together; a few small feathers may be bound in to add a finished and Indian look to the bolas. To the ends of the strings attach the bullets

(**FIG. 11-17**). To cast the bolas, grasp it by the feathered part with the thumb and first finger, whirl it around your head as you would an ordinary sling. When you let go, the loaded ends of the strings will fly apart, so that the missile will cover a space in the air of five feet in diameter. If a string strike a bird it will instantly wrap itself round and round the body; if the loaded end strike the game it will, of course, stun or disable it. One of these instruments cast into a flock of birds is certain to bring down several.

For target practice, use in the place of the ordinary butt a number of reeds or sticks stuck upright in the ground about a foot apart; after measuring the distance for the marksman to stand and marking the spot, let him see how many reeds he can level at a single cast of the bolas. The one who makes the biggest score can assume the title of "Big Injun," and wear a feather in his hat, or an appropriate badge, until some more skilled hand beats the record and wins the title and the badge. No shots should count unless made in a regularly appointed match.

The Elastic Cross-Bow (A New Kind of Cross-Bow)

Select a piece of thick pine or cedar plank and saw out a piece of the form shown by A, **FIG. 11-18**. Trim it down with a jack-knife until it becomes more finished and gun-like in appearance. With a gouge, such as may be borrowed at any carpenter or cabinet-maker's shop, cut a half round groove from the butt to the muzzle of the barrel. The groove must be perfectly straight and true (B, **FIG. 11-18**). Bore a hole in the piece (E), for the bow to fit in. The bow in this case should be made perfectly stiff, so as not to bend in the least when the line is drawn and the gun set. The bow may be bent into the proper form by steeping it in boiling water until the wood becomes pliable, and binding it

FIG. 11-18

The Elastic Cross-Bow

firmly into the required position. After it has become perfectly dry the wood will retain the form and the bindings may be cut off. Trim the bow nicely into shape, and make it of such size that it will *not bend* when the string is drawn. Fit the bow into place, not like an ordinary crossbow but in a reversed position, as shown by the diagram C, **FIG. 11-18**. It might be an improvement to set the bow back toward the stock an inch or two further than the one in the illustration. For a bow-line use two pieces of strong elastic: with a string for a centre piece. The centre cord prevents the bow-line from wearing out as soon as it would if it were all elastic (**FIG. 11-18**, C). Make the trigger in the manner described for the plunger pistol (**FIG. 12-4**, page 137), but instead of fastening it upon one side with a screw, set it in a slot cut for the purpose in the middle of the barrel near the stock, and let it move freely upon a pivot. Cut a thin, smooth piece of pine just long and wide enough to cover the gun-barrel from stock to muzzle, and fasten it on with a couple of small brads at the muzzle and a screw at the stock (**FIG. 11-18**, C).

FIG. 11-19

Elastic Sling

Hunter's Cabin

There is always a certain amount of danger attending the use of firearms which is avoided by the cross-bow, added to which advantage is the fact that the twang a bowstring makes is so slight a noise as not to alarm the game, and if the young sportsman be inexperienced he may shoot several times at the same bird or rabbit without frightening it away. With a little practice it is astonishing what precision of aim can be obtained with the cross-bow. I know boys who seldom miss a bird even with the simple elastic sling, consisting of two pieces of rubber bands attached to a forked or a straight stick (**FIG. 11-19**).

CHAPTER 12

HOW TO MAKE BLOW-GUNS ELDER GUNS, ETC.

THE fierce and savage head hunters of Borneo go to war armed with the same implements with which the school-boys shoot peas or pellets of clay at unsuspecting citizens as they pass the ambuscade of tree or fence. The blow-guns used by the Dyaks of Borneo are called sumpitans, and instead of clay balls they carry poisoned arrows. A spear is also attached to the side of one end of the sumpitan, after the manner of a bayonet on a modern rifle. In speaking of the sumpitan a recent writer says: "This curious weapon is about eight feet in length and not quite an inch in diameter, and is bored with the greatest accuracy, a task that occupies a long time, the wood being very hard and the interior of the sumpitan smooth and even polished. It is not always made of the same wood. The surface is of equal thickness from end to end." Among the South American Indians the sumpitan is represented by the long delicate "pucuna," or the heavy and unwieldy "zarabatana." All savages use poisoned arrows in their blow-guns instead of harmless pellets of clay or putty. Taking a few hints from the primitive warriors and hunters of Borneo and South America, any boy, with a little care and small expense, can construct for himself a blow-gun which will be handy to carry around and will shoot with great accuracy. Mr. W. Hamilton Gibson, the well-known artist, has acquired such skill with the blowgun that he seldom misses the mark, and often brings home birds and other creatures brought down by a clay pellet blown from a glass sumpitan.

For twenty-five cents a glass tube, three or four feet long, can be purchased. With these tubes can be made the best of blowguns, but they are objectionable on account of being liable to break at any moment from some accidental blow or jar. With some flannel or woollen cloth and an old piece of cane fishing-pole a cover and a case can be made to enclose the glass and prevent its being broken by anything short of a severe knock or fall.

To Make a Blow-Gun

Select a good straight piece of glass tube about three or four feet long. To discover whether the glass tube is straight or not, hold it horizontally level with the eye and look through it, and any deviation will be quickly seen. Wrap the tube with strips of flannel or woollen cloth, as illustrated by **FIG. 12-1**, A. The cloth will make a soft covering or cushion for the outside of the glass and render it less liable to break. With a red-hot iron rod, or some similar instrument, enlarge the hollow in the centre of a piece of cane until the blow-gun can be slid inside the cane. With putty, shoemakers' wax or beeswax secure the tips of the tube in place. Trim off the ends of the cane until they are flush with the ends of the glass. You will then have a blow-gun that can be used to hunt with (B, **FIG. 12-1**). For missiles may be used arrows, tacks, peas, or clay. The arrows must be very small, and a pin with its head filed off makes a simple point; some raw cotton bound on the butt end to make it fit the inside of the gun finishes the missile (**FIG. 12-1**, D). The tack is prepared by fastening short pieces of

FIG. 12-1

The Hunter's Blow-Gun

worsted or carpet ravellings to it just below the head with shoemakers' or beeswax (C, **FIG. 12-1**).

This not only fills up the space inside the blow-gun, making it fit, but the yarn also acts as a feather does upon an arrow and causes the tack to fly straight and point foremost. The worsted-headed tack is a "tip-top" missile for target practice. The clay pellet will bring down small birds, stunning them, but doing them no serious injury, so that if the birds are quickly picked up they can be captured alive.

Along the Mississippi River, from New Orleans to Nashville, there are still some remnants of the Indians that in olden times paddled their canoes up and down the Father of Waters. The boys among these tribes make splendid blow-guns out of cane. When the inside is bored out they straighten the cane by heating it over hot coals, and then, after attaching a heavy weight to one end, suspending it by a string attached to the other end. The heat from the hot coals makes the cane pliable, and before it becomes cold and hard, the weights make it almost as straight and true as a rifle-barrel.

Squirt-Guns

Some time during the summer of each year a boy used to appear with a squirt-gun made of a piece of cane. Squirt-gun-time then commenced, next day four or five guns might be seen on the play-grounds, and before a week had passed the curbstone in front of the little frame school-house presented a line of boys all busily engaged in seeing who could shoot the greatest distance; the dusty macadamized street registered every drop of water by a muddy spot. I found that by adding a quill as a nozzle to my "squirt" it would throw water much further than the others. It is a very simple thing to make a good squirt-gun, and one may be manufactured in a few minutes.

First cut a joint from a piece of an old cane fishing-pole, being careful not to disturb the pithy substance that almost closes the hollow at the joints. Insert a quill for a nozzle at one of the joints and see that it fits tightly; leave the other end open. With your pocket-knife fashion from a piece of pine or cedar the plunger (B, **FIG. 12-2**); leave the wood a little thicker at both ends and wrap a rag around one end, making it just thick enough to fit snugly in the cane after wetting it. This completes the "squirt" (A, **FIG. 12-2**). To use it, immerse the quill in water, first push the plunger in, then draw it out slowly until the gun is filled with water. Take aim, and when you push the plunger back again the water will issue from the quill in a sudden stream, travelling quite a distance. One of these water-guns is quite useful in the garden; by its means the insects infesting the rose bushes and other shrubs may be knocked off in no time. When the owner of an aquarium finds dead animals or plants that should

FIG. 12-2

Cane Squirt-Gun

be removed, located in some crack or cranny that is difficult to reach, the squirt-gun is just the thing to dislodge the objects without disturbing the surrounding rocks or plants.

Elder-Guns and Pistols

When the author was a very small boy he was taught by some playmates to make an elder gun, a simple contrivance, made of a piece of elder or any other hollow stick. A long notch cut in one side admits a spring made of whalebone (**FIG. 12-3**). By pushing the spring back the short arrow shown in the illustration can be propelled quite a distance. If instead of the awkward whalebone spring a piece of elastic be used, a much neater gun can be made. **FIG. 12-4** shows a pistol made with an elderbarrel and a stock of pine. A plunger, similar in many respects to the

FIG. 12-3

A Simple Elder-Gun

one used in the squirt-gun, is made with an edge to catch in the trigger. An elastic band is bound to the barrel with string, and the loop fastened to the butt end of the plunger. When the latter is drawn back to the trigger it stretches the elastic. By pulling the trigger toward you it loosens the plunger, which flies back with a snap, sending the arrow out with considerable force.

FIG. 12-4

Plunger Pistol

The barrel of the pistol may be fastened to the stock by two strips of tin or leather. The diagram shows the form of the trigger, which should be made so as to move readily backward or forward upon the screw that fastens it to the stock. **FIG. 12-5** shows how a pistol can be made to work without a plunger. In this case the barrel is partly cut off from A to B. The arrow should be made to fit in the groove, so that when the elastic is loosened it will strike the arrow in the same manner that the string of a cross-bow does. Both these pistols, if made with good, strong

FIG. 12-5

Pistol without a Plunger

elastic, will shoot quite a distance, and if the arrows are armed with a tack or pin in the head they can be used in target practice. We now come to a gun in which the spring is the principal part.

The Spring Shot-Gun

A certain old gentleman was at one time very much annoyed by fine bird-shot which at all times of the day came rattling against the window-panes of his study. Being somewhat of a philosopher, the old man at last became deeply interested in investigating the cause of his annoyance.

From the window he could see a house separated from his study by a deep backyard, a vacant lot, and another yard. While peering out between the blinds of his window he saw a boy appear at one of the windows of the distant house; the boy held something in his left hand which he pulled with his right; almost instantly there was a rattling of bird-shot against the old gentleman's window glass, and the boy disappeared. But so great was the distance that separated the two houses that it was impossible for the old man to distinguish what sort of an instrument the mischievous lad used to propel the fine shot so far and with such force. The youngster was at last waylaid, and the mystery solved. The machine used proved to be a spring shot-gun. No powder or explosive is used with one of these guns, neither does it possess stock, trigger, or sights, but simply consists of a stick of whalebone or any other elastic material, one end of which is armed with a large quill, corked at its lower end.

FIG. 12-6

Spring Shot-gun

When the quill is filled with fine bird-shot and the end of the stick grasped by the left hand, the contents of the quill can be thrown an amazing distance by bending the quill end back and allowing it to suddenly fly forward, upon the principle of the whip bow. If instead of a small piece of whalebone a large and very elastic rod be used, with a tin tube in the place of the quill, an effective weapon will be produced useful for hunting and collecting purposes; although the shot cast from the tube will have sufficient force to stun a small bird, it will not injure the specimen by making ugly holes in the skin and staining the feathers with blood. All of the weapons described in this and other chapters should be used with care, for many of them are capable of inflicting severe wounds. Never aim a bended bow with arrow set at a companion or friend, for a little slip may cause irreparable harm. Even a blunt arrow propelled from a barrel-hoop bow has sufficient force to destroy an eye or make a severe bruise. A true sportsman has the greatest respect for his weapons and handles them with scrupulous care.

CHAPTER 13

TRAPS
AND TRAPPINGS

SUMMER is over. Again the air becomes cooler. The straw hats are discarded, so also are the linen suits; we begin to look up heavier clothing, for although the sun still shines brightly, the nights are growing chill. Even at midday we no longer seek the shady side of the streets or the roadways.

In the woods all the little inhabitants are preparing for the approaching winter. Backward and forward, from the beech tree to his nest under the wood-pile, runs the nimble little brown-coated, striped-back chipmunk, each trip adding to the pile of beech nuts secreted in the storehouse of this provident little fellow. Scampering along the top rail of the fence the gray squirrel may be seen, also busily engaged in laying up a supply of winter stores. The birds are gathering in large flocks, with noisy twitterings and excited flutterings, preparatory to their yearly pilgrimage to the Sunny South. The bouncing hare is thinking of discarding its summer coat of brown and donning its white winter furs. The leaves of the ivy vines shine like red fire wreathed around the tree trunks. All nature seems busy going through a transformation scene—an air of preparation is visible everywhere.

The reports of the sportsmen's guns may be heard, and their dogs may be seen in the stubble-fields manoeuvreing like well-drilled soldiers promptly obeying every command of their masters.

And far and wide—in the cold Northern regions, in the pine woods of Maine, in the Rocky Mountains of the West—the hardy trappers are busy collecting their traps and making preparations, or are already engaged in their annual campaign against all fur-bearing animals.

In order that my reader may not be behind the season, this chapter is devoted to the description of a few simple but effective traps and snares, such as may be made of the material always at hand, with the aid of a pocket-knife, hatchet, or other tools within the reach of boys.

Rats

We have in North America more than fifty kinds of rats and mice, the largest of which is the muskrat. Next in size comes the great, ugly brown rat.

More than three hundred years ago the black rat found its way from Europe to this country, settled here with our ancestors, and, like them, increased and prospered. The black rat is rather a neater and prettier animal than the now omnipresent Norway brown rat. The latter is of Asiatic origin, and appears to have made its way to this country since the advent of the black rat, which it has supplanted and almost exterminated. The roof rat in the Southern States came originally from Egypt, and the little brown mouse that creates so much mischief in our closets is of Asiatic parentage. All rats may be caught in traps, and for an amateur trapper the house rat is a good subject to practice on. By no means a fool among animals, possessing a due regard for his own safety, and looking with suspicion upon most traps, the Norway brown rat is not so easily caught as one who has never baited a "figure four" might suppose. A very successful way to capture house rats is to carefully close all the doors of the kitchen, barn, or room infested with them, and after removing all small objects from the floor, bait each hole with crumbs of meal and cheese; over the holes place little doors made of tin or wire, hung on with strings or screw-eyes, these doors open but one way and are so arranged that the rat can easily push the door open from the inside, but as soon as the animal makes its appearance in the room the door falls back into place, thus cutting off all retreat. In a short time the room will be overrun with rats, and if allowed to remain undisturbed for a few hours they will all escape through new holes made by their sharp teeth; if a terrier dog or a few cats be let into the room, not many rats will live to tell the tale of the massacre.

A Mouse Trap

The Paper Pitfall

Over the top of an earthenware jar fasten a piece of writing paper, tightly binding it with a string or elastic band. In the centre of the paper cut a cross as shown in the illustration (**FIG. 13-1**). Set the jar in the closet and suspend by a string a piece of toasted cheese over the centre of the jar. If there are any mice in the closet the bait will attract them, but just as soon as the first mouse reaches the centre of the paper he will drop into the jar, and the paper will fly back in place again ready for the next comer. A trap arranged in the same manner can be used for the capture of field mice, shrews, and harvest mice, some of which make odd and amusing pets. All of these pretty little animals may be found in the fields or under brush heaps in the clearings. A barrel covered with stiff brown paper can be used for common rats, but they will gnaw out unless the barrel be partly filled with water.

Jug Trap

An old earthenware jug with a small hole knocked in the upper part may be utilized as a trap for small burrowing animals. Bury the jug in the earth (**FIG. 13-2**) near the haunts of the animal you are after; then

FIG. 13-2

Old Jug Trap

arrange an artificial burrow extending from the surface of the ground to the hole in the broken jug; strew appropriate bait along the passageway, and although the little creatures might hesitate to enter a broken jug above ground, they are said to have no fear of one beneath the sod, and either jump or fall inside, where they may be allowed to remain some time with no fear of their escaping.

The jug trap is only suitable for small animals.

The Mole and How to Trap Him

Moles are, generally speaking, harmless creatures who render the farmer a great service by devouring immense quantities of grubs and larvæ; but when one of these little animals finds its way under the sod of the lawn it plays sad havoc with the looks of the grass, furrowing the surface with ridges, and marring the appearance by dirt hills.

From the fact that the mole travels under ground, I have spent considerable time in trying to find a trap to catch this subterranean animal. Among we boys that lived in the valley of the Ohio River, a mole skin was highly prized as a sort of fetich that, when used as a "knuckle dabster" to rest our hands on in a game of marbles, not only prevented our hands from becoming soiled—which was no great matter—but also insured good luck to the happy boy who possessed a knuckle dabster made of a mole skin. There are but very few animals that can boast of fur as soft and fine as that which covers the back of the common mole.

A mole trap can be made in the old reliable figure four style, with which most of my readers are no doubt familiar.

The Figure Four

is made of three sticks; a catch-stick, A, an upright, B, and a trigger, C (**FIG. 13-3**). When these sticks are set in the position shown by the diagram, and a weight allowed to rest on the top of the catch, A, the sticks will keep their positions and support the weight until the trigger, C, is touched.

FIG. 13-3

Construction of the Figure Four

At the slightest derangement of the trigger all the sticks fall, and the weight above, being left without a support, instantly drops to the ground. This trap has been ingeniously adapted to the purpose of a

Mole Trap

A heavy weight is fastened on a piece of plank or board for a deadfall; in the centre of the board some sharp-pointed spikes or nails are driven, so that the pointed ends extend several inches below the deadfall (see **FIG. 13-4**). This trap should be set over a fresh mole-way, no bait need be used.

First press down the loose earth in a line across the ridge, then set the trap with a figure four, allowing the trigger-stick to rest in the place where you have pressed down the earth across the mole hill. The trap should be so arranged that the sharp spikes will be directly over the hill. The next time the mole makes his way through the underground passage he will sooner or later come to the place where the earth has been pressed down to make room for the trigger.

FIG. 13-4

Mole Trap

When the little animal reaches this point and proceeds to loosen the earth again, the movement will displace the trigger and bring the dead weight down, pinioning the mole to the ground with the sharp spikes, to which the loose earth of the mole hill offers but little resistance, if the weight be heavy enough. If the skin of the animal be desired, it is best to use as few spikes as practicable, for the fewer holes there are in a pelt the more valuable it is.

I object to deadfalls on principle, and it is not without some reluctance that I include them among the traps. As a boy, the only traps I ever used were made for capturing animals alive; but there are occasions when it is perfectly proper to use a deadfall. If the animal sought is a nuisance upon whose extermination you have settled for good reasons, then use a deadfall, or if you desire the animal for food and have no other means of capturing him, the deadfall is very convenient. Supposing your supply of fresh meat has run short at camp, or that you are on a canoe trip and are placed under similar circumstances, if there be a rabbit or squirrel in the neighborhood no one will find fault with you for trying to capture the game by any means in your power.

The Toll-gate Trap

is so called either from its resemblance to a toll-gate, or from the fact of its being set across the top of a rail fence, which has been called the "squirrel's highway." This trap can be made in a few minutes with the aid of a pocket-knife and a hatchet. The toll-gate is a deadfall, and the little traveller pays the toll with his life. With your hatchet cut a forked stick and drive it in the ground a few feet from the fence; rest one end of a plank on this forked stick and allow the other end to protrude some distance beyond the opposite side of the fence. Select a heavy stick for the deadfall, and a very much smaller stick for the trigger; near the end of the trigger cut a notch for the catch-stick to rest in. Sharpen the ends of two small forked sticks and drive them into splits made near the ends of the board with the corner of the hatchet. Lay a cross piece from one forked stick to the other, and with a bit of string or vegetable fiber suspend the catch-stick from the centre of the cross stick. Tie the inside end of the trigger loosely to the deadfall, and adjust the trap so that when the end of the deadfall rests upon the catch-stick the latter will hold the trigger an inch or so above the plank. To prevent the trap from swaying and to

Toll-gate Trap

guide the deadfall in the proper direction, two upright guide-sticks should be erected (**FIG. 13-5**). The weight of a squirrel's foot upon the bottom bar slips it from the catch-stick and down comes the deadfall upon the shoulders of the victim.

This same style of trap may be made upon a much larger scale and set on logs or trees that have fallen across a watercourse and are used as a bridge by minks, 'coons, or other animals. The forked sticks supporting the end of the plank must in this case be driven into the bed of the creek, and a plank twenty feet long substituted for the short one used in the trap designed for squirrels.

To be a successful trapper a boy must be a keen observer of the habits of the game; by this means he will soon learn to take advantage of the very means designed by Nature as a protection for her creatures. For instance, the partridges are not good flyers, but their unobtrusive coats mingle and blend so closely with the stubble as to take a sharp eye to detect their presence; hence we find that these birds are loth to take to the wing, but will run along any slight obstruction they meet, poking their heads about to find an outlet, apparently never once thinking of surmounting both the difficulty and the obstruction by using their wings. The "down East" Yankee boys are thoroughly acquainted with the habits of the partridge, and catch a great many of them by building, little hedges like the one in the illustration entitled

The Partridge Snare

The snare in this case consists of a slip-noose made of string. Make a bow-line knot (**FIG. 1-4**, diagram XIII., described on page 8) in one end of a piece of common string or fish line; slip the other end of the string through the loop and make the free end fast to the top of an arch made of a bent stick (see **FIG. 13-6**). In a semi-circular form, around some feeding ground, build a low fence of sticks, brush or stones, leaving openings at intervals only large enough to fit in arched gateways. Make an arch for each opening and arrange a slip-noose in each archway; spread the loops apart and keep them in this position by catching the strings slightly into notches made upon the outside of the arch (see **FIG. 13-6**). The birds, when they seek their accus-

FIG. 13-6

The Partridge Snare

tomed feeding place, will walk into the semi-circle, and in searching for an outlet they will go poking their heads about until they come to an archway; here they thrust their heads through the slip-noose, and as, instead of backing out, a partridge will try to force its way through, the noose tightens and holds the bird a prisoner. Sometimes the youthful trapper will find the lifeless body of a rabbit with the fatal noose around its neck, and often he will miss one or two of his arches that have been uprooted and carried away by large game becoming entangled, and walking off, carrying arch, noose, and all with them. This partridge snare will also catch quail or prairie chickens.

Set-Line Snares

Snares when used for catching birds alive should be closely watched; which will not only prevent the captured wild birds from beating themselves to death, but will save them from suffering any more pain than is absolutely necessary.

Select a smooth piece of ground and drive two stakes; to these attach a long cord, allowing it to stretch loosely upon the ground from one stake to the other. At intervals along the line fasten strong horse-hair nooses (**FIG. 13-7**). Sprinkle food around and retire out of sight to watch. When the birds discover the food they will collect around it, and some one of them is almost certain to become entangled in one of the snares. As soon as a bird is snared it should be disentangled and put into a covered basket or a paper bag; pin-holes may be made in the bag to allow the air to enter. In this way birds may be carried home without injury; being in the dark they are not likely to hurt or disfigure themselves by struggling for their liberty. A cage is not only an awkward, unwieldy contrivance to carry in the field, but is objectionable from the fact that a wild bird caught and thrust into a cage will bruise its head and wings badly by striking against the bars in the efforts it makes to escape. Paper bags, pasteboard boxes, or covered baskets will do to carry home captured wild birds in.

FIG. 13-7

Set-line Snares

The Spring Snare

Make a low arch by pointing both ends of a stick and forcing them into the ground. Cut a switch and bend it into the form of a lawn tennis racket, and with a string fasten the small end of the switch to the part that answers to the handle of the bat or racket; just beyond the point where the small end terminates cut a notch in the large part or handle for the catch-stick to fit in. Make a short stick, with one end wedge-shaped, for a catch-stick. Drive a peg at such a distance in front of the arch that when the loop of the spreader is slipped over the peg the notch on the butt end will come just far enough to allow the catch-stick to hold it, as in **FIG. 13-8**. For a spring use an elastic young sapling.

After stripping off the leaves and branches, attach a line to the top, tie the other end of the line to the catch-stick, and just above the cross stick fasten one end of a slip-noose to the line. To set the snare, bend the sapling until you can pass the catch-stick under the bender or arch, **FIGS. 13-8**. Raise the spreader from the ground about an inch; let the catch-stick hold it in this position, and spread the slip-noose over the loop-stick; your trap is now ready. To attract the birds, scatter some appropriate bait inside and very little outside. The birds will follow the trail of food up to the stretcher, and seeing the bait inside will hop upon the stretcher preparatory to going within. The stretcher, being only supported by friction where it bears against the catch and peg, will drop under the weight of a very small bird. The catch loosened slips out from under the bender, and the spring flying suddenly back draws the slip-noose around the wing, legs, or neck of the unfortunate bird. Unless speedily released by the trapper the bird will strangle or beat itself to death against the ground, or any objects within reach. *All snares should be watched if the birds are wanted alive.*

Hen-Coop Trap

FIG. 13-9

Hen-Coop

This rustic trap is sometimes set with an ordinary figure four (**FIG. 13-3**) by the colored people down South, and with it they catch a great many wild ducks and other water fowl.

The coop is made of sticks piled up after the manner of a log cabin (**FIG. 13-9**). To one of the bottom sticks a withe, made of a green wand,* is attached; the other end is then brought over the top of the trap and attached to the bottom stick upon the opposite side. The withe is tightened by forcing sticks under it at the top of the coop. When all is taut the sticks keep their positions, and unless very roughly used will not slip out. **FIG. 13-10** shows another manner of setting the hen-coop trap, by fastening a piece of willow or any other similar wood by two strings or withes to one end of the coop,

FIG 13-10

Hen-Coop Trap

so as to allow considerable freedom of motion to the semi-circular arch formed by the willow, which should be small enough and bent in such a manner that all parts of the arch will come inside the coop. Take two forked sticks and make the straight part of one of such a length that it might support one end of the coop. Cut one of the forks off the second stick and leave about two inches of the other fork on (see D, **FIG. 10-10**). Make B about an inch shorter than A (**FIG. 13-10**). Raise the side of the coop, thrusting the crook on the end of B through the fork on the end of A, slip the crook under the edge of the coop, and push the bottom of B back inside of the willow, lifting the latter high enough to bear on the stick B and hold it in position. A will rest outside the coop, as in the illustration. A bird hopping upon the willow wand will cause it to slip down; this will displace the stick A, loosen the catch, and down comes the coop, enclosing the bird. A rustic trap of this description can be made without the aid of any other tools than a hatchet or a knife for cutting the sticks.

---

* Withes may be made of ozier, willow, alder, hazel, white birch, white cherry, or even cedar branches

Cut a branch or sapling, and after trimming the small branches off, place the small end under one foot, grasp the large end with both hands, and by a revolving motion twist the wand until the fibres become loosened and the stick looks like a rope. Indeed it will be a vegetable rope, which, if well made, will bear considerable strain, and be not only serviceable in making traps, but answer for binding logs together for a raft. Remarkably good and strong swings can be made of withes of wood.

CHAPTER 14

DECOYS

Top View of

BEFORE writing further in this line, the author must confess that as a boy or man he never killed an animal without a feeling of remorse for what he had done, and it was only after long thought and study upon this subject that he decided to put anything about hunting and trapping in this book. But after mature deliberation, the conclusion reached was that other boys must have the same sensations as himself, when a bloody little trophy of their skill is stowed away in their game-bag, and that these feelings will prevent the average lad from killing for the sake of killing; for there is no fun in wanton destruction of life for a properly educated boy; and the writer trusts that none of his readers will ever aim their guns at a harmless song-bird, or any other creature not considered necessary for the table. And now that we understand one another, let us see if we cannot also understand the game.

Top View of Duck-frame

FIG. 14-1

FIG. 14-2

Dead Duck Decoys

As the triangle of the wild ducks in the sky approach their feeding-ground, and catch sight of their fellows, already at their repast, they argue, and rightly so, that there can be no enemy near.

Hunters and sportsmen, being well acquainted with this fact, go to the resort of the ducks, and scatter over the water a lot of frauds in the shape of ducks made of wood to deceive the wild birds overhead; but these have the usual objection that most boys find to all hunting apparatus— expense. Now, if my reader is an expert, and can slip up within range and secure a duck or two, he can, with little trouble, convert the dead ducks into decoys to lure on their live comrades to death, and the place of honor on the dinner table.

With your pocket-knife cut four pieces of wood in the proportions shown in **FIG. 14-1**; bind them together with string, take a small switch, and bend it in a loop as a support for the tail, and fasten it in place, as shown in the diagram. At what might be termed the bow, fasten an upright Y-shaped stick, or a sharp pointed one to hold the dead duck's head in place. Two pointed sticks fastened in the sides will keep the bird in place.

FIG. 14-2 shows a side view of the duck frame. A string is attached to one end with a stone for an anchor; it keeps the head of the decoy to the wind, after the manner of a live duck, and the live bird will not discover the cheat until it is too late to retreat, provided the reader is a good shot. **FIG. 14-3** shows the dead duck set up as a decoy.

FIG. 14-3

Shingle Snipe and Plover Decoys

The diagrams, **FIGS. 14-4**, **14-5**, **14-6**, explain the construction of these decoys so well that it is only necessary to say that they can be made of shingles by the aid of your pocket-knife, and, with some paint added, will look enough like the real birds to deceive even the much-persecuted and wary snipe and plover.

The second (**FIG. 14-5**) shows one with wings of birch bark added. **FIG. 14-6** gives the pattern of the birch-wings.

To be a good hunter it is absolutely necessary to be well posted upon the habits of the creature hunted; and such a person will secure game where another person would not even suspect its presence.

Place your decoys for snipe in the muddy or marshy spot that the birds are wont to frequent; then hide in some convenient blind or cover. Of course, a top view of the shingle decoy presents only a straight line to the eye, as does a direct end view; but this matters little, as these particular views are not the ones likely to be seen by the birds, especially if there is a number of decoys set at different angles.

FIG. 14-4

FIG. 14-5

Shingle Decoy - - - - With wings

The Wings

FIG. 14-6

PART V
THE BOY INVENTOR

CHAPTER 15

BIRD SINGERS
MUSIC
AND NOISE MAKERS

VERY many amusing contrivances can be made of the most simple materials. I have seen boys pluck a blade of grass, and, by simply stretching it edgewise between their thumbs, make a musical instrument with which they could imitate the notes of a singing bird so closely as to perfectly deceive persons not in the secret. After placing the blade of grass, as shown by the illustration (**FIG. 15-1**), put your lips to your thumbs at the hollow between the joints and blow. The result will be a shrill noise which, with very little practice, can be made to resemble the notes of different wild birds.

FIG. 15-1

FIG. 15-2

The Block Bird Singer

The illustration (**FIG. 15-2**) shows an instrument made upon the same principle as the "bird singer" just described. The "block bird singer" consists of two blocks of pine small enough to fit between the front teeth of the operator. The blocks are hollowed out in the middle, as shown by A, **FIG. 15-2**.

Stretch a blade of grass across the hollow of one of the blocks and place the other block on top of it, as shown by B, **FIG. 15-2**. Place the blocks between your teeth, and by drawing in and expelling your breath you can produce a series of shrill noises which, with practice, may be made to imitate the notes of a singing bird. A thin strip of writing-paper may be substituted for the blade of grass where the latter is hard to procure.

The Corn-stalk Fiddle

The writing of the above title has sent me back to my boyhood with one great leap over the intervening years. In imagination I am again a barefooted youngster, with straw hat, short pants, and checked apron. Again I can experience the feeling of pride and importance as from my pocket comes the well-remembered jack-knife, with a great shining blade that opens, like any *man's* knife, with a snap! If I were this moment placed in a particular barn-yard in company with my reader, I could take him to the exact spot

FIG. 15-3

Cornstalk Fiddle

where a pile of corn-stalks used always to be heaped up in the corner of the fence. Let us suppose we are there. Select a good straight corn-stalk, and with the "shiny" blade of the jack-knife cut four slits from joint to joint, as shown by the top diagram, **FIG. 15-3**. Now out of that chip at your feet make a wooden bridge like the one shown by A, **FIG. 15-3**. With the point of the jack-knife lift up the three strings of the fiddle and slide the bridge under them edgewise; then gently, but firmly, raise it to an upright position and spread the strings apart, allowing them to fit into the notches cut for the purpose in the bridge (see lower diagram, **FIG. 15-3**). Make the bow of a smaller corn-stalk than that used for the fiddle. No tune can be played upon this instrument, but a funny squeaking noise can be produced.

The squeak of the corn-stalk fiddle brings to my mind another rustic instrument.

The Pumpkin-vine Fife

Cut a good thick, straight pumpkin-stem and make holes in it like those in a fife. If you know how to blow on a fife you may not only produce a noise with the pumpkin-stem, but a tune may be played upon this simple instrument which, even if only partially successful, will amuse your hearers to that degree that you will feel yourself amply repaid for the trouble.

A Pumpkin-vine Flute

Cut off a long leaf-stem like the one shown in the illustration (**FIG. 15-4**). With the blade of your knife make a slit (A, B) through both sides of the stem. Then at the base of the leaf, in the solid part just beyond the end of the hollow in the stem, cut off the stem at C, D. By putting this end in the mouth and blowing, a noise will be produced, deep and sonorous, sounding like a distant steam-boat's whistle. Holes may be cut for the fingers similar to those just described for the fife.

If one stem fails to work, cut another and try it until you succeed. The pumpkin-vine flute, like the corn-stalk fiddle, will amuse small boys, but if my reader does not belong to that class he may make of a piece of fishing-cane a first-rate fife.

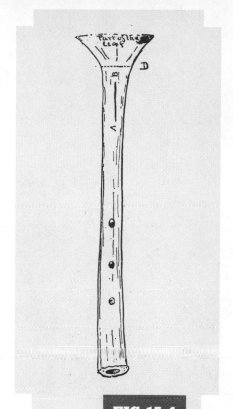

FIG. 15-4

A Pumpkin-vine Flute

The Voice Disguiser

is made of a piece of corn-stalk about three inches long. After removing the pith cut a notch near each end, as shown in the illustration (**FIG. 15-5**), upon opposite sides of the corn-stalk; upon the ends stretch a piece of fish-bladder, or any thin membrane; a piece of thin tracing-paper will answer.

FIG. 15-5

Voice Disguiser

FIG. 15-6

The Locust Singer

With a large pin make a hole in each piece of membrane, as shown at A in the illustration. Now cover the notch, cut into the corn-stalk, with your mouth and laugh; the noise you produce will set you laughing in earnest. By placing your mouth over either of the notches and talking or singing, the voice is so changed as to be perfectly disguised, and if you sing a song through this instrument it sounds like some one playing on a comb covered with paper. The voice disguiser is very handy in Punch and Judy or puppet shows.

The Locust Singer

This little instrument, simple as it is, is calculated to afford considerable amusement.

With one of these toys can be made not only a loud noise, which in itself pleases most boys, but it reproduces exactly the sound of the *cicada,* or "locust," as the harvest-fly is commonly but improperly called. The "locust singer," as may be seen by reference to the illustration (**FIG. 15-6**), consists of a horse-hair with a loop at one end and a weight attached to the other end. A pine stick, with a groove cut around it near the top, is thrust through the loop of horse-hair, and the groove in the stick thickly covered with powdered rosin.

When the weight is swung rapidly around, the horse-hair, in sliding over the rosined stick, produces a noise which closely resembles the well-known song of the harvest-fly. If a tin pillbox is used for a weight and the hair run through a hole in the lid and fastened by a knot upon the inside, the lid of the box acts as a sort of sounding-board. A piece of parchment or paper is sometimes pasted over the box tightly, like a drum-head, and the hair attached to this; but a little stone wrapped in a piece of cloth answers every purpose.

A piece of kid, from a discarded glove, tied tightly over the top of a bottle-head, makes a loud-voiced locust singer. The head of the bottle may easily be removed, by striking repeated blows with a case-knife on the neck of the bottle, at the desired point of separation.

How to Make an "Uncle Enos" Banjo

FIG. 15-7 shows a cigar-box, with holes bored through the ends for the sticks that supports the neck to pass through. The bottom of the box is used for the top to the banjo. The lid of the box may be left on, so that it can be closed or opened, as the taste or ear of the banjoist may direct.

FIG. 15-8 represents a pine board with a plan of the neck drawn upon it, ready to be sawed out. *D, d', d'', d'''* mark the spots where holes are to be bored through for the key to turn in. The place for the low bridge that separates the strings before they enter the keys is marked by the dotted lines at *a*; a rectangular slot should be cut here to fit the bridge (**FIG. 15-9**, 5) into, as shown by the side-view of the neck (**FIG. 15-10**); *b* (**FIG. 15-8**) is a keyhole in the side of the neck for the short string. See side-view (**FIG. 15-10**).

The slot for a small bridge for the short string of the banjo is marked by the dotted line at *c* (**FIG. 15-8**). This little bridge is fitted in the slot, as shown in the side-view (**FIG. 15-10**).

FIG. 15-8

FIG. 15-9

FIG. 15-10

FIG. 15-11

FIG. 15-11 shows the broomstick, whittled down at one end, so as to fit the holes bored in the cigar-box, through which it must pass and protrude about one-half inch at the butt. The top to the upper part of the broomstick is smoothed off flat, so that the neck (**FIG. 15-8**) may be securely screwed on to it, as is more clearly shown by the side-view (**FIG. 15-10**).

FIG. 15-9, 4 shows what shape to make the keys. The latter must have holes (just large enough for the banjo strings to pass through) bored near the ends, as shown in the diagram. The keys may be made of any kind of wood—hard wood is the best.

FIG. 15-9, 5 shows the bridge that fits into the slot *a* (**FIG. 15-8**), already described.

FIG. 15-9, 6 is simply a piece if tin bent into the shape shown in the diagram, and made to fit over the butt-end of the banjo for the wires of **FIG. 15-9**, 7 to pass over when the latter is put in place (see **FIG. 15-12**).

FIG. 15-9, 7 is a piece of hard wood of leather with five small holes bored through it for the attachment of the banjo-strings, and a wire loop at the end that passes over the piece of tin (**FIG. 15-9**, 6), and is held in place by the tension of the strings and the protruding end of the broomstick at the butt of the banjo (**FIG. 15-12**).

The bridge proper is shown by **FIG. 15-9**, 8. It may be cut from a piece of soft pine in a few moments, with a pocket-knife. Its place is in front of **FIG. 15-9**, 7, where it spreads the five strings before they pass over the head and neck of the instrument.

FIG. 15-10 shows the neck finished and all ready to be fitted to the box. The neck is fastened to the broom-stick support by two screws, as may be seen in the diagram.

FIG. 15-12 shows the finished instrument, all strung and ready for use.

FIG. 15-13 shows the arrangement of the banjo strings. The shortest string on the banjo is the fifth. And now we have reached the part where the boy who wants to make an Uncle Enos banjo will have to expend a few cents. Go to a dealer, and for the first and fifth ask for E strings. Let the first be little heavier than the fifth. The second should also be an E string, but much heavier than the first. For the third, ask for a guitar B string. The fourth, or bass string, is manufactured especially for the now popular banjo, and care must be taken not to purchase the guitar D for the banjo A, or bass; both strings are silver, wound on silk, but the latter is much finer wound than the guitar D.

The author has seen a banjo under the direction of his old friend Uncle Enos, and the whole thing cost but half a day's labor and forty cents for strings.

FIG. 15-12

FIG. 15-13

CHAPTER 16

THE
WATER-TELESCOPE

GLASS

Bottom!

NEARLY three-fourths of the whole world is covered by water. Old Isaak Walton in his quaint book says that this vast expanse of territory is "Nature's storehouse, in which she locks up all her wonders." The later chapters on fresh water and marine aquariums will show how a portion of the "wonders" may be kept in your own house, in what might be termed little glass side-shows to the great marine menagerie. This chapter will tell you how to make an instrument through which you can peep under the watery tent of the big show itself, and see the curiosities swimming about in their native haunts.

The water-telescope is not made of aqueous fluid, as its name might imply, but is a contrivance made of wood or metal, through which, when one end is partly submerged, objects beneath the water can be plainly seen that would otherwise be invisible.

It is astonishing how many fathoms of water become almost as transparent as air when viewed through one of these simple and amusing contrivances. In Norway, the fishermen make practical use of the water telescope when searching for herring shoals or cod, often by its means discovering new and unlooked-for fish.

How to Make a Wooden Water-Telescope

All that is necessary is a long wooden box, a piece of glass for one end, and some paint and putty for making the seams water-tight. Fix the

FIG. 16-1

Wooden Water-Telescope

glass in one end of the box, and leave the other end open to admit the eyes of the observer, as shown in the illustration (**FIG. 16-1**).

A Tin Water-Telescope

A Tin Water-Telescope is a funnel-shaped tin horn, about three or four feet long, eight to ten inches in diameter at the bottom, and broad enough at the top to admit both eyes of the observer (**FIG. 16-2**). Sinkers should be soldered on near the bottom, as shown in the illustration (**FIG. 16-2**). This in a measure counteracts the buoyancy of the air contained in the water-tight funnel, and helps to submerge the big end.

The inside of the funnel should be painted black, to prevent the light from being reflected upon the bright surface of the tin.

If any difficulty is found in procuring a circular piece of glass, the bottom may be made square and square glass used, and fitted into a leaden frame made for the purpose.

FIG. 16-2

A Tin Water-Telescope

Any tinner can, at a moderate cost, make an instrument like the one just described.

A water-telescope will add greatly to the entertainment of a boating party or picnic, furnishing a new and novel feature that will become popular wherever it is introduced.

Mr. Fred Holder tells me that while collecting marine animals with his father, Dr. Holder, the naturalist, they had a boat built with a glass in the hull, arranged and worked upon the same principle as a water-telescope. It was of great service where the water was not too deep. While one person rowed the other watched the bottom, which Mr. Holder describes as having the appearance of a beautiful panorama passing beneath him. Fish of all colors and forms filled the intervening space, and sometimes a "devil fish" would cross the scene, flapping its great wing like fins as it flew rather than swam through the clear water.

CHAPTER 17

FOURTH OF JULY BALLOONS
WITH NEW AND NOVEL ATTACHMENTS

How to Make a Fourth of July Balloon

Did you ever, while watching a beautiful soap-bubble dance merrily through the air, think how closely it resembled the immense silken bubble beneath which the daring aëronaut goes bounding among the clouds?

Especially is this true of the gas-bubble described in the foregoing chapter. When a boy, the author's ambition naturally led him from these vapor balloons to experimenting in more lasting material than soapsuds. He then devoted his attention for some time to paper balloons, and, after numerous experiments and disasters, succeeded in building balloons of a style which is comparatively safe from accident and seldom the cause of a mortifying failure. If you do not want to disappoint the spectators by having a fire instead of an ascension, avoid models with small mouth-openings or narrow necks. Experience has also taught the writer that balloons of good, substantial, portly build go up best and make their journey in a stately, dignified manner, while the slim, narrow balloon, on the contrary, even if it succeeds in getting a safe start, goes bobbing through the air, turning this way and that, until the flame from the fire-ball touches

FIG. 17-1

Regular-shaped Balloon (safe)

171

FIG. 17-2

*Too long a neck
(unsafe)*

FIG. 17-3

*Too Square and
Narrow (unsafe)*

FIG. 17-4

Too Narrow (unsafe)

and lights the thin paper, leaving only a handful of ashes floating upon the summer breeze.

The reader can see here illustrated some of the objectionable shapes as well as some of the safe styles. For large balloons, strong manila-paper is best; for smaller ones, use tissue-paper.

When you build a balloon, decide first what height you want it; then make the side pieces or gores nearly a third longer; a balloon of thirteen gores, each six feet long and one foot greatest width, when distended with hot air ready to ascend, is a little over four feet high. For such a balloon, first make a pattern of stiff brown paper by which to cut the gores. To make the pattern, take a strip of paper six feet long and little over one foot wide; fold the paper in the centre length-wise, so that it will be only slightly over a half foot from the edges to the fold. Along the bottom measure two inches from the fold and mark the point. At one foot from the bottom, at right angles from the folded edge, measure three inches and one-half, and mark the point; in the same manner mark off five inches from two feet up the fold. From a point three feet four inches from the bottom measure off six inches and mark the point; from this place the width decreases. At the fourth foot mark a point five inches and one-half from the fold; about three inches and a third at the fifth foot; nothing, of course, at the sixth foot, or top, where the gore will come to a point. With chalk or pencil draw a curved line connecting these points; cut the paper along this line and unfold it.

You will have a pattern the shape of a cigar, four inches wide at the bottom, one foot greatest width, and six feet long. After pasting your sheets of manila or tissue-paper together in strips of the required length cut out thirteen gores by the pattern just made; lay one of these gores flat upon the floor, as in **FIG. 17-8**; fold it in the centre, as in **FIG. 17-9**; over this lay another gore, leaving a margin of the under gore protruding from beneath (**FIG. 17-10**). With a brush cover the protruding edge with paste, then turn it up and over upon the upper gore, and with towel or rag press it down until the two edges adhere. Fold the upper gore in the centre as you did the first one, and lay a third gore upon it; paste the free protruding edge; and so on until all thirteen are pasted. It will be found that the bottom gore and top gore have each an edge unpasted; lay these two edges together and paste them neatly.

Next you must make a loop of rattan or some light substance to fit the mouth opening, which will be about one foot and a half in diameter. Fasten the hoop in by pasting the edges of the mouth opening around it. In very large paper balloons it is well to place a piece of string along the edge of each gore and paste it in, letting the ends of the strings hang down below the mouth; fasten the hoop in with these ends before pasting the paper over it. It will be found next to impossible to tear the hoop from a balloon, strengthened in this manner, without totally destroying the balloon.

Should you discover an opening at the top of your balloon, caused by the points not joining exactly, tie it up with a string if it be small, but if it be a large hole paste a piece of paper over it. When dry, take a fan and fan the balloon as full of air as you can, and while it is inflated make a thorough inspection

FIG. 17-5

Round Balloon (safe)

FIG. 17-6

Slightly Elongated Balloon (safe)

FIG. 17-7

Pumpkin-shaped Balloon (safe)

Single Gore

FIG. 17-9

Single Gore Folded

FIG. 17-10

Folded Gore with a second Gore over it, ready for Pasting

of all sides to see that there are no accidental tears, holes or rips.

FIG. 17-11 shows the cross wires that support the fire-ball. The latter is best made of old-fashioned lamp-wick wound rather loosely, in the form of a ball, the size depending upon the dimensions of the balloon. The sponge commonly used soon burns out and the balloon comes down in a very little while; but the wick-ball here described seldom fails to propel the little air-ship upward and onward out of sight. A short, fine wire should next be run quite through the wick-ball, so that it can be attached to the mouth of the balloon in an instant by hooking the ends of this wire over the cross wires at the mouth.

If you use a little care you will have no difficulty in sending up the balloon. Place your wick-ball in a pan or dish, put the corked bottle of alcohol beside it, and about thirty feet away make a simple fire-place of bricks or stones, over which place a piece of stove-pipe. Fill the fire-place with shavings, twisted pieces of paper, or anything that will light readily and make a good blaze. In a loop of string fastened at the top of the balloon for that purpose let one of the party put the end of a smooth stick, and, with the other end in his hand, mount some elevated position and hold the balloon over the fire-place. Before touching a match to the combustibles below, expand the balloon as much as possible by fanning it full of air; then light the fire. Be very careful, in all the process that follows, to hold the mouth of the balloon directly above and not too near the stove-pipe, to prevent the blaze from setting fire to the paper, which will easily ignite. At this stage of the proceedings one person must take the bottle of alcohol, uncork it, and pour the contents over the wick-ball in the basin, and the ball must be made to soak up all it will hold of the spirits. The balloon will become more and more buoyant as the air becomes heated inside, and at length, when distended to its utmost, it will begin pulling to free itself. Holding the hoop at the mouth, walk to one side of the fire and with all speed have the ball attached securely in place. Touch a light to it, and it will blaze up. At the words "All right," let go. The same instant the stick must be slid from the loop on top, so as not to tear the paper, and away will sail the balloon upon its airy voyage.

Never attempt to send up a balloon upon a windy day, for the wind will be sure, sooner or later, to blow the blaze aside and set the paper on fire, and if once it catches up in the air there is not much use in trying to save it.

After you have made a balloon like the one just described and sent it up successfully, you can try other shapes. A very good plan in experimenting is to make a small working model of light tissue-paper, fill it with cold air by means of an ordinary fan, and when it is expanded any defect in form or proportion can be readily detected and remedied. If it be too narrow, cut it open at one seam and put in another gore, or *vice versâ,* until you are satisfied with the result; with this as a pattern, construct your larger balloon. Such a model, eighteen inches high, lies upon the writer's table. He has sent it up in the house several times by holding it a few moments over a burning gas-jet. The balloon rapidly

FIG. 17-11

Top view of Hoop and Cross Wire, Wick-ball and Side view of Hoop showing Wick-ball hung in place

FIG. 17-12

Method of pasting Paper and Strings for Parachute

FIG. 17-13

*Parachute attached
to the Fuse and Wire*

FIG. 17-14

The Car

fills with heated air, and when freed soars up to the ceiling, where it rolls along until the air cools, then falls gently to the floor.

Balloons with Parachutes

The parachute shown in the tail-piece is simply a square piece of paper with a string at each of the four corners, meeting a short distance underneath, where a weight is attached. **FIG. 17-12** shows how to make one that will not tear. It is made of two square pieces of paper. Two pieces of string are laid diagonally across the first paper; on top of this the second piece of paper is pasted, enclosing the strings without disturbing them; the ends of the strings come out at the corners.

These parachutes are attached to a wire that hangs from the balloon in this manner: From the centre and top of the parachute is a string, we will say, a foot long; this is tied securely to one end of the large fuse from a pack of Chinese fire-crackers; a few inches from the other end of the fuse another string is tied and fastened to the wire. Just as the balloon starts the free end of the fuse is lighted (**FIG. 17-13**). When it has burned itself away past the point where the lower string has been fastened, it of course severs the connection between the parachute and the balloon, and the parachute drops, but does not go far, before the air beneath spreads it out, the weight at the bottom balances it, and it floats away slowly, settling lower and lower, but often travelling miles before finally reaching the earth.

All manner of objects may be attached to a parachute—notes addressed to possible finders, letters, or figures of men or animals. The latter look very odd in the air.

A real passenger balloon may be very closely imitated by painting crossed black lines upon the upper part of a paper balloon to represent the net-work. A pasteboard balloon-car, made after the manner shown in **FIG. 17-14**, and holding two pasteboard men cut out as shown in **FIG. 17-15**, may be hung on by hooking the wires attached to the car over the hoop at the mouth of the balloon. When the balloon and car are a little distance up in the air, it takes a sharp eye to detect the deception, because distance in the air cannot be easily judged.

But so far we have dealt only with day balloons; for night, you must attach some luminous object.

A lantern made like the one described in "Kite-time" (**FIG. 26-29**) may be fastened to the balloon by a long string and wire, and when it goes swinging after the larger light above, it has a curious appearance. In a similar manner, a long string of lanterns may be hung on to a large balloon, or packs of Chinese crackers may be exploded in mid-air by means of a fuse.

The writer has experimented in other fireworks, but found them very dangerous to handle. Mr. Stallknecht, of the *Hat, Cap and Fur Trade Review*, however, showed the author how to make a simple, safe, and beautiful pyrotechnic out of a Roman candle with colored balls, a piece of wire and a fuse. The fuse used can be bought

FIG.17-16

Night Balloon

FIG. 17-17

in almost any city or town; it is sold to miners for setting off blasts. With the wire make a sort of wheel, with two or three spokes; cut open the Roman candle and extract the powder and balls; wrap up each ball with some of the powder loosely in a piece of tissue-paper and tie the paper at the ends upon the spokes or cross wires of the wheel, as shown in **FIG. 17-17**. Run the fuse spirally around, passing through each parcel containing a ball, and allow the long end of the fuse to trail down beneath from the centre or side (**FIG. 17-18**). To the rim of the wire wheel attach several wires of equal lengths with hooked ends; hook these on to the hoop at the mouth of the balloon just before letting it go, and light the trailing end of the fuse. As the fire creeps slowly along, the balloon mounts higher and higher. Suddenly the whole balloon glows with a ruddy, lurid glare. The fire has reached the first ball. In another instant you see a floating globe of pale green light, then blue, and so on, until all the balls are consumed. Showers of pretty, jagged sparks are falling constantly during the illumination, caused by the burning powder. By the time all is over the tiny light of the solitary ball in the balloon looks like a star in the sky above, travelling where the wind chooses to blow it. The most experienced aëronaut has but very little more command over the actions of his immense silken airship than has the young amateur who builds his balloon of tissue-paper and sends it skyward with a ball of fire for its motive power.

FIG. 17-18

Paper Fire-works

Simultaneously with the announcement in the New York City papers that by an explosion of red fire the author of this book had met with a terrible accident, and the probable loss of his eyesight, there appeared in the Youths' Companion, an article by the injured party on "Harmless Paper Fire-works."

If the author had confined himself to his own suggestions he would have just as much or more enjoyment, saved himself a terrible ordeal, and six months' loss of time, besides saving his friends from the anxiety they felt over the doubtful recovery of his sight. And here he wants to thank the number of boys, strangers to him by name, but whose friend-ship he values and evidently possesses, for their very kind letters during his temporary blindness, which letters he was unable to answer on account of the red fire having, for the time being, closed and sealed those wonderful little curtains we call eyelids.

FIG. 17-19

Paper Thunderbolts

do not, as might be inferred from their name, make noise, but silently dart about in the sky as a most novel and amusing manner.

When Mr. W. Hamilton Gibson occupied the studio at 191 Broadway, and the author was a travelling surveyor, Mr. Gibson used to amuse himself and friends by making these thunder-bolts and dropping them from the window of his studio.

Cut some colored paper into pieces about four inches wide and eight inches long. Then at one end of the each piece cut it into strips about one-third of the length of the paper (**FIG. 17-20**). Pinch the uncut end of the paper together, and twist it tightly, so that it will not come undone (**FIG. 17-21**).

FIG. 17-20

FIG. 17-21

The Fuse

FIG. 17-22

If one can be procured, buy a miner's fuse; if not, soak a piece of loosely twisted twine or cord in wet gunpowder and allow it to dry, or use the focus from the centre of a pack of fire-crackers.

Make a bundle of a hundred or more various-colored thunderbolts, wrap them loosely in a piece of tissue-paper, and bind them with a piece of twine which has first been tied to the fuse, about an inch or two from the end of the latter, in such a manner that the inch or two of fuse forms part of the band around the thunderbolts (**FIG. 17-22**), while the rest of the fuse is left free (D to B, **FIGS. 17-22–17-23**).

Then make fast the loose end of the twine to your big Fourth of July kite's tail (E, **FIGS. 17-22–17-23**). Send up the kite, and, just as she rises, light the free end of the fuse, and as the kite ascends the fuse will burn slowly up to the bundle until it reaches the part where it forms part of the band around the thunderbolts. As soon as it burns here the weight of the bundle severs the charred band, and down come all the odd-shaped pieces of paper, darting this way and that, and all of them acting as if possessed with life, presenting not only an amusing but a really beautiful sight in the sky.

Parachutes

FIG. 17-23

If a number of simply made parachutes be attached to the powder-soaked string, at intervals, as the fuse burns to the point of attachment, they will drop off, and float away in the most graceful and beautiful manner. Make the parachutes of tissue-paper cut into pieces about five inches square. Twist each corner, and fasten to it a thread about eight inches long (**FIG. 17-24**). Wrap a small pebble in pieces of scrap-paper, and make it take the form of a torpedo: make the four free ends of thread fast to the pebble (**FIG. 17-25**). A twist in the centre of the paper will give a point to attach the thread to (**FIG. 17-25**), the other end is fastened to the fuse (**FIG. 17-23**).

FIG. 17-24

FIG. 17-25

CHAPTER 18

HOW TO MAKE
A MAGIC LANTERN
A KALEIDOSCOPE

A Home-made Magic Lantern

Upon opening his eyes late one summer morning the author was very much startled and astonished at an apparition he beheld upon the wall. He saw at one side of the room, in a waving circle of light, a horrible gaping monster that was about to make a mouthful of a wriggling, big-headed creature, as large as a cat. Upon turning over in bed and facing the window, the cause of this strange phenomenon was seen. The "gaping monster" proved to be a tiny gar, and the wriggler nothing more nor less than a tadpole. The curtains of the window had fallen down upon each side of a glass globe in which some aquarium pets were quarrelling. A ray of the morning sun had found its way into the darkened room through the fish globe, and by some unaccountable means transformed the globe into a sort of magic lantern lens and slide, throwing the magnified reflections of the inmates of the aquarium upon the wall. The gradual change in the position of the sun caused the vision to fade away in a few moments, and the writer has never since been able to arrange the light so as to reproduce the same effect. Fortunately, however, some one else has discovered the principle, and from it evolved a simple magic lantern, which any boy can make for himself; an account of this invention lately appeared in the *Scientific American,* and the editors of that paper have kindly consented to allow the description to be used for the benefit of the "American Boys."

FIG. 18-1

A Magic Lantern

All that is required for this apparatus is an ordinary wooden packing-box, A (**FIG. 18-1**), a kerosene hand-lamp, B, with an Argand burner, a small fish globe, C, and a burning-glass or magnifying-glass (a common double or plano-convex lens), D. In one end of the box, A, cut a round hole, E, large enough to admit a portion of the globe, C, suspended within the box, A, with the lamp, B, close to it. The globe is filled with water, from which the air has been expelled by boiling.

Now moisten the surface of a piece of common window-glass with a strong solution of common table salt, dissolved in water, and place it vertically in a little stand made of wire, as shown at F, so that the light from the lamp, B, will be focused on it by the globe, which in this case answers as the condenser. The image of the glass will then be projected on the wall or screen of white cloth, G, providing the lens, D, is so placed in the path of the rays of light as to focus on the wall or screen. In a few minutes the salt solution on the surface of the glass, F, will begin to crystallize, and as each group of crystals takes beautiful forms, its image will be projected on the wall or screen, G, and will grow, as if by magic, into a beautiful forest of fern-like trees; it will continue to grow as long as there is any solution on the glass to crystallize. Then by adding a few drops of any transparent color to the water in the globe, the image on the screen will be illumined by shades of colored light. If the room in which the experiment is performed be very cold, frost crystals can be made by breathing on the glass, F. Many other experiments will suggest themselves, and when tried will be found both entertaining and instructive.

A Home-made Kaleidoscope

At all glaziers' shops there are heaps of broken glass, composed of fragments of what were once long strips, cut with the diamond from pieces of window-pane, when fitting them for the sash. If you secure three of these strips of the same size, and tie them together in the form shown by **FIG. 18-2**, the strings will keep the glass in position. Cut a piece of semi-transparent writing-paper in the form shown by **FIG. 18-3**, so that it will fit on one end of the prism. With mucilage or paste fasten the overlapping edges to the glass; then with dark or opaque paper make another piece to fit upon the opposite end of the kaleidoscope; the opaque end-piece should have a round hole in its centre about the size of a silver twenty-cent piece—this is for the observer's eye. All that now remains to be done is to cover the sides of the apparatus with the same paper used for the eye-piece, and the kaleidoscope is finished.

FIG. 18-2

Kaleidoscope

Drop a few bits of colored glass, beads or transparent pebbles in and turn the writing-paper end to the light; place your strings will keep the glass in position. Cut a piece of semitransparent writing-paper in the form shown by **FIG. 18-3**, so that it will fit on one end of the prism. With mucilage or paste eye at the hole cut for that purpose in the opaque paper end, and as you look keep the prism slowly turning; the reflection in the glass will make the objects within take all manner of ever-changing, odd, and beautiful forms. A kaleidoscope made in the manner described is as serviceable and produces as good results as one for which you would have to pay several dollars at a store. One of the home-made ones can be manufactured in ten minutes if the pieces of glass be of the same length, and need no trimming to make them even.

FIG. 18-3

*End Piece of
Kaleidoscope*

CHAPTER 19

HOW TO MAKE VARIOUS AND DIVERS WHIRLIGIGS

WHO can watch machinery of any kind in motion, without experiencing an indefinable sort of pleasure? No matter how simple the contrivance may be, if it move it immediately interests us. This instinct, if I may so call it, that prompts us to watch and play with machinery is implanted in the brain of the lower animals as well as of man. I think no one can doubt that a kitten or a dog enjoys chasing a ball, and enters into the sport with as much zest as a college-boy does his game of football. It is this same indefinable desire for observing and experimenting with moving objects that prompts us to throw stones for the purpose of seeing them skip over the surface of the water, and to this instinct must be attributed the pleasure experienced by the school-boy with his

Potato Mill

which consists of simply a stick, a potato, a buckeye, or a horse-chestnut, and a string. The stick is whittled into the form shown in the illustration; a string is fastened to the stick about one-half inch below the knob on the top. The buckeye has a large hole bored through the middle, and a small hole bored through one side, to the middle hole; the string from the stick passes through the hole in the side of the buckeye; the end of the stick is sharpened and thrust into a potato.

FIG. 19-1

The Potato Mill

If the string be wound around the stick, and the buckeye held between the thumb and forefinger, the stick and potato may be made to spin rapidly by alternately pulling the string and allowing it to slacken; the motion imparted by the first pull continues long enough to wind the string in the opposite direction, and thus, for an indefinite time, or until the string wears out by friction, the potato mill may be kept buzzing at a great rate.

Another machine the boys used to be very fond of was called

A Saw-Mill

it was generally made out of the top of a tin blacking-box, with the rim knocked off and the edge cut into notches like a saw. Two strings passing through two holes near the centre gave a revolving motion to the "buzzer" (**FIG. 19-2** shows a saw-mill). By holding the strings so that the wheel hangs loosely in the middle, and swinging the wheel or "buzzer" around and around until the string becomes tightly twisted, the machine is wound up. As with the potato mill, the revolving motion is imparted by alternately pulling and allowing the string to slacken, only in this case you must hold one end of the string in each hand (**FIG. 19-2**). When the boys can make a buzzer actually saw into a piece of board

FIG. 19-2

A Saw-Mill

or shingle by allowing the edge of the wheel to strike the wood, the saw-mill is pronounced a success, and its value increased.

Very pretty and amusing toys may be made on the same principle as the saw or potato mills described. One of these little machines, a very fascinating one, is sold upon the streets of New York by the novelty peddlers. As the writer was passing along Broadway the other day, he saw an old acquaintance, known to almost all New Yorkers by the name of "Little Charlie." Little Charlie is not a small man, as his name might imply, but a large, good-natured, red-faced peddler, who stands all day long at the street corners. During the winter he sells small india-rubber dolls, crying out to the passers-by: "Well! well! well! Little Charlie! double him up! double him up!" He doubles the little india-rubber dolls up in a comical manner to attract customers. The torrid summer heat is too much for the india-rubber dolls, and makes them sticky, so that they are laid aside during the hot weather, and Little Charlie, with the perspiration streaming from his face, no longer calls out in his accustomed manner, but stands silently twirling his summer novelty, trusting to the ever-changing colors of the toy to attract purchasers. One was bought that it might be introduced among the other whirligigs in this chapter.

A disk of the Rainbow Whirligig

The Rainbow Whirligig

If you have a pair of dividers, make a circle upon a piece of card-board about two inches in diameter; inside this circle make six other circles (**FIG. 19-3**). A pair of scissors can be made to do the duty of a pair of dividers by spreading them apart the required distance and thrusting the points through a card to hold them in position (**FIG. 19-4**). Make a duplicate figure or disk and paint the parts of the inside circles, shaded in the diagram, different colors; for instance, A and D may be made blue, B and E green, C and F red. The points of the star in the centre made by the intersection of the circumference of the circles should be painted the same color as the parts of the circle adjoining. Upon the second disk paint A and D blue, B and E yellow, C and F red.

Cut a piece of one-quarter inch pine into a square, with sides of about two and one-quarter inches in length; cut off the corners as shown by I, **FIG. 19-5**. In a hole in the centre of I fasten

A pair of Dividers

FIG. 19-5

Parts of Rainbow Whirligig

tightly the round stick J. Whittle out another piece for a handle K, and bore a hole through the top for the stick J to fit in loosely; bore another hole through one side for the string to pass through. In the illustration, as in the original from which the drawing was made, there is a large hole bored through two sides; but this is unnecessary, and only put in the diagram to better show the position of the string inside. Upon the wooden plate I, describe a circle about one and three-quarter inches in diameter. In the centre of the two paper disks make holes large enough to fit with shoe-eyelets; then with tacks (L, **FIG. 19-5**) fasten the two paper disks on to the wooden plate at the points G and H, in such a manner that the tack passing through the eyelets will allow the disks to revolve freely. Attach a string to the stick J at a point that will come opposite the string-hole in the side of the handle, when the stick J is slid into the hole at the top of the handle K. The wooden disk is made to spin exactly in the same manner that motion is imparted to the potato mill already described. When in motion the colors on the paper disks will blend and produce, with each change of position, a number of beautiful variations. The two paper disks blend together, making a large circle three and one-half inches in diameter, composed of concentric rings of the most lovely hues—red, pink, purple, green, and all the different shades and combinations imaginable are portrayed with ever-changing variety by the spinning rainbow whirligig.

FIG. 19-6

Paradoxical Whirligig

A Paradoxical Whirligig

is a very ingenious toy, consisting of a circle of white card-board, upon the surface of which any number of black rings are painted, one within the other, until it resembles an archery butt or target.

The disk is tacked or glued securely to a stick or handle (**FIG. 19-6**) so that it is impossible for it to really revolve, yet if you grasp the toy by the handle and give your arm a motion similar to that of the shaft of an engine, the disk upon the stick will appear to revolve like a wheel, and so closely does the optical delusion resemble actual motion that it will deceive almost any one who is not familiar with the experiment.

A picture of a wagon, with wheels made like the disks of the paradoxical whirligig, may be made, and the wheels will have all the appearance of revolving when a wabbling motion is imparted to the picture. There are many curious experiments that can be tried in this line—spirals may be made to twist around; pictured machinery may be given the appearance of actual moving wheels, etc. The philosophy of all this is best explained in the description of the next whirligig.

The Phantasmoscope, or Magic Wheel

The phantasmoscope, or magic wheel, is comparatively simple, consisting, as may be seen by the accompanying illustration, of a disk of any diameter revolving upon a pin in the centre. Figures in different poses of arrested action are painted or pasted upon the one side; under each figure is an oblong opening or slot. Much amusement can be derived from this old and simple toy. We herewith give one with the correct positions of a horse trotting a 2:40 gait, drawn in silhouette upon the outer margin of the wheel.

Make a careful tracing of the illustration (**FIG. 19-7**) with a lead-pencil upon tracing-paper; reverse the tracing-paper upon a piece of card-board so that the side with the pencil-markings on it will be next to the card-board; after which fasten both card-board and paper to a drawing-board or table-top with tacks, so that neither tracing nor card-board can slip. With the point of a hard pencil, a slate-pencil or any similar instrument, go carefully over each line of the tracing as seen through the tracing-paper; be careful not to omit a single mark; it is very

FIG. 19-7

The Magic Wheel

provoking to discover, after removing the tracing-paper, that part of the drawing is wanting; but if you have been careful, when the tacks are removed you will find the picture neatly transferred on the card-board. Go carefully over each line on the card-board with a pen and black ink, and fill in the outlines of each picture with ink, making a silhouette of the figures.

Cut the phantasmoscope, or magic disk, out, following the outer circle with the scissors, and under each figure, where the oblong places are drawn, cut a corresponding opening through the pasteboard. Fasten the wheel to a stick or handle by means of a pin at its centre, on which it can freely turn.

To use the magic wheel, stand in front of a mirror, as shown in the small illustration; hold the disk before the eyes; look through the slots under the figures, and turn the wheel rapidly. The horses' legs will commence to move as in life, and as each successive position drawn upon the phantasmoscope is the exact one taken by a trotting horse, the horses in the mirror will all appear to be in actual motion, on a fast trot. If the eye is directed over the margin of the paste-board disk, an indistinct blur is all that is seen. The principle is generally well known and easily explained. It pertains to the phenomenon known as the persistence of vision. When the eye is directed through the slot, the figure of a horse is seen for an instant as the opening passes the eye, and the impression is retained after the object is shut off by the intervening portion of the board between the slots until another horse appears through the succeeding opening, when an additional impression is made, the same as the preceding impression, except a slight change in the position of the legs. These impressions follow each other so rapidly that they produce upon the retina of the eye the effect of a continuous image of the horses, in which the limbs, replaced by a succession of positions, present the appearance of a file of horses in actual motion.

FIG. 19-8

Making the Horses Trot

The instantaneous photographs taken nowadays of people, horses, and other animals in motion, open a new field for investigation, and one which, with the aid of the simple toy described, will be found very entertaining as well as instructive.

Mr. Muybridge's celebrated photographs of animals in motion can all be adapted by smart boys to home-made phantasmoscopes, and it will probably not be long before the wonderful photographs of birds and bats on the wing, taken by E. J. Marcy with his revolving photographic gun, will be within reach of the public. Then with the magic disk the reader can make birds fly, horses trot, men ride bicycles, and reproduce every movement as correct as in nature.

For young scientists these beautiful experiments will be found very entertaining.

CHAPTER 20

THE UNIVERSE IN A CARD-BOX

A jovial-looking commercial traveller once won a wager from the landlord of a certain Detroit hotel by making over a hundred rings with one mouthful of smoke. The writer was sitting in the hotel office at the time, and becoming interested in the conversation, watched to see how the trick was done. Taking some cards from his card-case, the young man proceeded to bend up the edges in such a manner that the centre part of each formed a perfect square. Six cards he folded in this manner; then, after fishing in his pockets for some time, he produced a dime and a lead-pencil. Placing the ten-cent piece upon the centre of one card, he made a ring with the lead-pencil by following the edges of the coin. Opening a pocketknife at the file blade, with the point he cut a round hole in the card, following the circle made by the pencil. He then put the cards together, in the form of a light but strong box

FIG. 20-1

Smoke-Rings

195

FIG. 20-2

FIG. 20-3

FIG. 20-4

FIG. 20-5

The Card-box

(**FIGS. 20-2**, **20-3**, **20-4** and **20-5**), and taking a long pull at a cigar which was between his lips, he filled his cheeks, and blew the smoke into the paper box. By this time all the idlers in the office had collected around the smoker, who, with a triumphant smile upon his face, commenced to tap the sides of the box with his lead-pencil. At each tap a tiny but perfect and beautiful ring of smoke shot into the air—one hundred and ten were counted before the smoke was exhausted. **FIG. 20-6** shows how similar rings can be made with a lamp-chimney in which a card disk with a hole in it has been placed; a piece of paper or membrane fastened over the other end serves for a vibrating surface, which, when struck with the thumb, forces out the little rings of smoke.

The reader must not for a moment suppose that it is necessary to use tobacco smoke to perform this beautiful experiment; any other smoke will answer just as well to make the "vortex rings," as they are scientifically called. If after dipping a paint-brush into india ink, or any water-color paint, you gently insert the tip of the brush into a glass of clear water, you will see the pigment fall from the end of the brush, and, gradually sinking to the bottom, form rings exactly similar to the circles of smoke described.

FIG. 20-6

Lamp-Chimney

The rings made by skipping a flat stone over the water are but another example of the vortex, and the jolly commercial traveller, when he was exhibiting the little paper box and smoke-rings to the laughing crowd of fellow-travellers in the hotel office, was standing upon the threshold of a mighty mystery, experimenting with laws, and showing the action of the same forces that are supposed to have produced the wonderful rings around Saturn! Indeed, it is asserted that the broad, misty band of light which we see at night stretched across the heavens, and known to every boy as the milky-way, is nothing more nor less than a gigantic vortex ring, composed of millions of heavenly atoms. Some very learned men think that the secret of the whole universe, the origin of gravitation and electricity, are all locked up in the mystery which controls the formation and motion of a simple smoke-ring.

As Adrien Guebhard wisely remarks, in an interesting article upon this same subject, "Nothing is vulgar to one who knows how to see, and nothing indifferent to one who knows how to observe."

PART VI
THE BOY NATURALIST

CHAPTER 21

HOW TO STOCK, MAKE, AND KEEP A FRESH-WATER AQUARIUM

ALTHOUGH marine animals may surpass the inhabitants of fresh water in strangeness of form and tint, there are some fresh-water fish upon whom Mother Nature appears to have lavished her colors; and there are enough aquatic objects to be found, in any stream or pond, to keep all my readers busy and happy for years in studying their habits and natural history. One must have a certain amount of knowledge of the habits of an animal before he can expect to keep it in a thriving condition in captivity. This knowledge is gained by observation, and success depends upon the common sense displayed in discreetly using the information thus obtained.

Aquariums

Do not make the common mistake of supposing that an aquarium is only a globe or ornamental tank, made to hold a few lazy gold-fish. Do not have china swans floating about upon the top of the water, nor ruined castles submerged beneath the surface. Such things are in bad taste. Generally speaking, ruined castles are not found at the bottoms of lakes and rivers, and china swans do not swim on streams and ponds. If you determine to have an aquarium, have one whose contents will afford a constant source of amusement and instruction—one that will attract the attention and interest of visitors as soon as they enter the room where it is. Sea-shells, corals, etc., should not be used in a fresh-water aquarium; they not only look out of place, but the lime and salts they contain will injure both fish and plant. Try to make your aquarium a miniature lake in all its details, and you will find the effect more pleasing to the eye. By making the artificial home of the aquatic creatures conform as nearly as possible to their natural ones you can keep them all in a healthy and lively condition.

At the bird-stores and other places where objects in natural history are sold, you may buy an aquarium of almost any size you wish, from the square tank with heavy iron castings to the small glass globe; the globes come in ten sizes.

Some time ago, when the author, then quite a small boy, was spending the summer upon the shores of Lake Erie, the older members of the household frequently went out on the lake after black bass, taking with them for bait a pail of the beautiful "painted minnows" found in the little brooks of Northern Ohio. Upon the return of a fishing party the minnows left in the pail were claimed by the children as their share of the spoils, but the little fish would scarcely live a day; in spite of all that could be done they would, one by one, turn upon their backs and expire. This was the source of much disappointment and remorseful feelings on the part of the children. One day half the minnows from the pail were poured into a large flat dish, that they might be better seen as they swam about; here they were forgotten for the time; on the morrow all the fish in the pail were found to be dead, but those in the flat dish were perfectly lively and well. This discovery led to a series of experiments which the author has continued at times up to the present date, and he feels no hesitancy in saying that, if the manufacturers of aquariums in this country had made it their object to build vessels in which no respectable fish could live, they could hardly have succeeded better, for they all violate this first rule: the greater the surface of water exposed to the air, the greater the quantity of oxygen absorbed from the atmosphere. Amateurs must bear in mind that "the value of water depends not so much on its bulk as on the advantageous distribution of its bulk over large spaces." In other words, flat, shallow vessels are the best.

In the light of this fact the author set to work to build his first aquarium. The materials for its construction were bought of the town glazier's son. The amount paid was several marbles, a broken-bladed Barlow knife, and a picture of the school teacher sketched in lead pencil upon the fly-leaf of a spelling-book. In exchange for these treasures, several fragments of window-glass, some paint, an old brush, and a lump of putty, was received. Two or three days' work resulted in the production of an aquarium. It was only twelve inches long, eight inches wide, and four inches high; but, although this tank was small, it was a real aquarium, and would hold water and living pets. A piece of glass 12 × 8 inches formed the bottom. The sides were fastened on by simply pasting paper along the outside edges; if left in this condition of course the water would leak through the cracks, soften the paper, and produce disastrous results.

To prevent this the cracks upon the inside were carefully puttied up and the putty covered with thin strips of glass, which the glazier good-naturedly cut for the purpose; this not only prevented the tank from leaking, but added greatly to its strength. The paper corners and all the outside, excepting the front was then covered with two or three coats of paint. The front glass was left clean for observation. A piece of pine board formed the base of the little aquarium. After it was carefully puttied around the bottom, where the glass set in the board, the latter was nicely painted to correspond with the rest of the structure, the whole was left to dry. Crude as this tank may appear from the description, it did not look so, and best of all it never leaked.

With a dip-net, made of an old piece of mosquito-netting, what fun it was to explore the spaces between the logs of the rafts in front of the old saw-mill! and what curious creatures were found lurking there! Little gars, whose tiny forms looked like bits of sticks; young spoon-bill fish (paddle-fish), with exaggerated upper lips one-third the length of their scaleless bodies; funny little black cat-fish, that looked for all the world like tadpoles, and scores of other creatures. Under the green vegetation in those spaces they found a safe retreat from the attacks of larger fish.

FIG. 21-1

Globe and Pump

If a constant supply of fresh water can be kept flowing in an aquarium, or the water constantly aërified by agitation, the ordinary misshapen tank may be run successfully. The glass globe, the most unnatural of all forms for aquariums, can be utilized in this way. There used to be in the window of a jewelry store, in an Ohio town, an ordinary glass fish-globe, in which lived and thrived a saucy little brook trout. Brook-trout, as most of my readers know, are found only in cool running water, and will not live for any great length of time in an ordinary aquarium. In this case, an artificial circulation of water was produced by means of a little pump run by clock-work. Every morning the jeweller wound up the machine, and all day long the little pump worked, pumping up the water from the globe, only to send it back again in a small but constant stream which poured from the little spout, each drop carrying with it into the water of the globe a small quantity of fresh air, including, of course, oxygen gas. (See **FIG. 21-1**.) And the little speckled trout lived and thrived, and, for aught I know to the contrary, is still swimming around in his crystal prison, waiting, with ever-ready mouth, to swallow up the blue-bottle flies thrown to him by his friend the jeweller. It is a great mistake to suppose that it is necessary to change the water in an aquarium every few days. The tank should be so arranged as to seldom if ever require a change of water. This is not difficult to accomplish.

If possible, have your aquarium made under your own eyes. Suppose you wish one, two feet long; then it should be sixteen inches wide and seven inches high; or 24″ × 7″ × 16″. Figure **21-2** shows an aquarium of the proper form and proportions. Figure **21-3** shows the popular, but unnatural and improper form. With a properly made aquarium, after it is once stocked with the right proportion of plant and animal life, there is no necessity of *ever* changing the water.

Both animals and plants breathe, and what is life to the plant is poison to the animal. Animals absorb oxygen and throw off carbonic acid gas; this gas the plants inhale, separating it into carbon and oxygen, absorbing the carbon, which is converted into their vegetable tissue, and throwing off the free oxygen for the animals to breathe. By having plants as well as animals in your tank, both classes are supplied with breathing material. When you start your aquarium, first cover the bottom with sand and gravel. Then build your rockery; it is better to cement it together and into place.

FIG. 21-2

FIG. 21-3

After this is all arranged, go to the nearest pond or brook, and dredge up some water plants. Any, that are not too large, will do—starwort, milfoil, bladder-wort, pondweed, etc. Fasten the roots of your plants to small stones with a bit of string, and arrange them about the tank to suit your taste. Fill the tank with water, and let it stand in the window for a week or two, where it will receive plenty of light and but little sun. By that time all your plants will be growing, and numerous other little plants will have started into life of their own accord. Then you may add your animals, and, if you do not overstock the tank, you need *never change the water*. Be sure not to handle the fish; if, for any cause, you wish to remove them, lift them gently with a dip-net.

Should you wish to keep a little turtle, a crawfish, or any such animal, you must have your rockery so arranged that part of it will protrude above the water; or, better still, have a vivarium or land-and-water aquarium, such as is shown in Figures **21-4** and **21-5**. With a tank made upon this plan you can have aquatic plants as well as land plants and flowers, a sandy beach for the turtle to sleep upon, as he loves to do,

FIG. 21-4

FIG. 21-5

and a rockery for the crawfish to hide in and keep out of mischief. Some species of snails like to crawl occasionally above the water-line. Such an aquarium makes an interesting object for the conservatory.

Figure **21-6** shows how a fountain can be made. The opening of the fountain should be so small as to allow only a fine jet of water to issue from it; the reservoir or supply-tank should be out of sight, and quite large, so that, by filling it at night, the fountain will keep playing all day. The waste-pipe should open at the level you intend to keep the water, and the opening should be covered with a piece of mosquito-netting or wire-gauze to prevent any creature from being drawn in.

In an aquarium with a slanting bottom, only the front need be of glass; the other three sides can be made of slate, which is also a good material for the false bottom. In ponds, rivers, and lakes, the only light received comes from above; so we can understand that a vessel admitting light upon all sides, as well as from the top, forms an unnaturally luminous abode for fish. The glass front is sufficient for the spectator to see through.

The author has a tank twenty-five inches long, eleven inches wide, and twelve inches high—far too narrow and deep; but these defects have been, in a measure, overcome by filling it only two-thirds full of water, and allowing the green vegetation to grow undisturbed upon three sides of the aquarium; the remaining side is kept clean by rubbing off all vegetable matter once a week with a long-handled bottle-washer.

A rag or a piece of sponge, tied upon the end of a stick, will answer the same purpose. This tank has been in a flourishing condition for three years, and the water has been changed only once, and then all the water was removed so that some alteration could be made in the rockery.

But one of the inmates has died since last summer, and that was a bachelor stickleback, who probably received a nip from the pincers of one of the craw-fish. Two of these creatures have their den in the rockery that occupies the centre of the tank. A German carp, from the Washington breeding-ponds, browses all day long upon the mossy surface of the rocks, or roots around the bottom, taking great mouthfuls of sand and then puffing it out again like smoke. A striped dace spends most of his time lying flat upon his stomach on the bottom, or roosting like some subaqueous bird upon branches of the aquatic plants or on a submerged rock. A big and a little "killie" dart around after the boat-bugs, which they seldom catch; and if they do, they drop them again in great trepidation. A diminutive pond-bass asserts his authority over the larger fish in a most tyrannous manner. An eel lives under the sand in the bottom, and deigns to make his appearance only once in several months, much to the amazement of the other inhabitants, all of whom seem to forget his presence until the smell of a bit of meat brings his long body from his retreat. Numerous little mussels creep along the bottom; periwinkles and snails crawl up and down the sides; caddice-worms cling to the plants, and everything appears perfectly at home and contented.

And why? Because their home is arranged as nearly as possible like their natural haunts, where they were captured. *Learn the habits of any creature, and give it a chance to follow them, and you will find little difficulty in keeping it healthy in captivity.*

FIG. 21-6

The Frog

For the benefit of the curious, here is a partial record of Mr. Frog's meals from May until November:

- **May 14th.**—Over a dozen brown beetles.
- **May 15th.**—One full-grown live mouse.
- **May 19th.**—One full-grown spotted frog.
- **May 24th.**—A piece of beef one-third size of the frog himself.
- **June 2nd, 9 a.m.**—One live mouse.
- **June 2nd, 1 p.m.**—One live mouse.
- **June 5th.**—A piece of steak one-half size of the frog.
- **July 18th.**—One full-grown live mouse.
- **July 20th.**—One young alligator 11¼ inches long.

This was a pet alligator, and I just came in in time to see the tip of his tail sticking out of the frog's mouth. Taking hold of the alligator's tail I helped Mr. Frog disgorge my pet, but the saurian was dead.

- **July 27th.**—One full-grown live mouse.
- **July 29th.**—One full-grown live mouse.
- **August 9th.**—One full-grown live mouse.
- **September 17th.**—One large brown bat.
- **September 20th.**—One live craw-fish.
- **September 21st.**—Two live craw-fish.
- **September 22nd.**—One live craw-fish.
- **September 25th, 27th, and October 8th.**
  —Each one full-grown live mouse.
- **November 15th.**
  —This gluttonous frog ate two-thirds of a white perch
- **November 17th.**—Died of a fit of indigestion.

But so celebrated had the frog become on account of his pluck and voracious appetite, that his obituary was published in several papers.

Craw-fish are very mischievous; they pull up the plants, upset the rockery, nip the ends off the fishes' tails, crack the mussel-shells, pull out the inmates and devour them, squeeze the caddice-worm from his little log-house, and, in fact, are incorrigible mischief-makers. But, from that very fact, I always keep one or two small ones. The other inhabitants of the aquarium soon learn to dread the pincer of these fresh-water lobsters, and keep out of the way. Tadpoles are always an interesting addition to an aquarium.

Pickerel and gars should be kept in an aquarium by themselves.

Pond-bass make very intelligent pets. I once had three hundred of these little fellows, perfectly tame. Down in one corner of the cornfield I found two patent washing-machines, the beds of which were shaped like scow-boats. These old machines were fast going to ruin, and I readily gained permission to use them for whatever purpose I wished; so, with a hatchet, I knocked off the legs and top-gear; then removed a side from each box, and fastened the two together, making a tank about four feet square. The seam, or crack, where the two parts joined, was filled with oakum, and the whole outside was thickly daubed with coal-tar. The tank was then set in a hole dug for

FIG. 21-7

Whirligig and the Eel

that purpose, and dirt filled in and packed around the sides. Back of it I piled rocks, and planted ferns in all the cracks and crannies, and also put rocks in the centre of the tank, first covering the bottom with sand and gravel. After filling this with water and plants, three hundred little bass were introduced, and they soon became so tame that they would follow my finger all around, or would jump out of the water for a bit of meat held between the fingers. Almost any wild creatures will yield to persistent kind treatment, and become tame. Generally, too, they learn to have a sort of trustful affection for their keepers, who, however, to earn the confidence of such friends, should be almost as wise, punctual, and unfailing as good Dame Nature herself.

CHAPTER 22

HOW TO STOCK, MAKE, AND KEEP A MARINE AQUARIUM

THE first introduction of the aquarium revealed another world and its inhabitants: a world of enchantment, far surpassing any described in the "Arabian Nights" or fairy tales; a world teeming with life so strange that some of it we can scarcely believe to be real.

The marine aquarium has laid bare secrets that have been looked in the breast of the ocean for ages. Through the crystal sides of the tanks are now shown living animals, of forms so lovely and delicate as to remind us of the tracery of frost-work. We can behold in the transparent waters fishes circling about, with distended fins that resemble the gorgeous wings of butterflies; and we can see, glancing here and there, other fish, the glitter of whose glossy sides dazzles us and is as various in hue as the rainbow. The rocks at the bottom are carpeted with animals in the forms of lovely flowers!

The remarks in regard to the form and general construction of fresh-water aquariums will apply equally to marine tanks. The best form for the latter is the shallow vessel with a slanting false bottom, described in a preceding chapter and illustrated by Figures **21-4** and **21-5**.

If you have a common rectangular tank, such as can be purchased at any aquarium-store (**FIG. 21-3**), it may be rendered inhabitable for marine animals by making a few improvements. Four tall glass panels admit too much light; therefore give the outside of the glass a coat of green paint on all but one side, leave that clean and transparent to serve as a window, through which may be observed the interior and its occupants. The rockery or arch that is to occupy the centre of the aquarium should be cemented together with marine cement. Although this is not absolutely necessary, it is the best plan, and prevents many accidents. The following receipt I cull from the *Scientific American*:

Cement for Marine Aquaria.—Take 10 parts, by measure, litharge, 10 parts plaster-of-Paris, 10 parts dry white sand, 1 part finely powdered resin, and mix them when wanted for use into a pretty stiff putty with boiled linseed oil. This will stick to wood, stone, metal or glass, and hardens under water. It resists the action of salt water. It is better not to use the tank until three days after it has been cemented.

The arch may be built out of clean cinders or ragged and irregular stones; an old oyster-shell with its rough side uppermost can be used as a top-piece. To make the arch steady and not liable to upset, the bottom should be composed of rather large flat stones.

Cover the bottom of the aquarium to a depth of an inch or more with sand from the beach. Procure the salt water from the ocean itself, and if possible obtain the supply some distance from shore. In no case must you dip the water for your aquarium up from the mouth of a fresh-water stream or muddy creek. If the tank is narrow and deep, fill only about one-third of it. Let the water stand in the aquarium for several days before introducing the plants. Select the bright algæ or seaweeds that you find attached to small pebbles; the stones will of course sink to the bottom of your aquarium and keep the plants in an upright and stationary position. After all is arranged to your satisfaction, choose a place for the location of your tank where there will be light enough to plainly see its contents and cause little bubbles of oxygen to collect and rise from the vegetation. A window facing the north or northeast is the best situation. When you observe that the plants are in a thriving condition, and that a new vegetation has apparently sprung spontaneously into existence, carpeting the rockery and sides of the glass with green, then and not until then introduce the animals. Be very careful not to overstock the tank. Remember, no matter how bright and pleasant a room may be with one or two persons in it, the atmosphere of that same room will become foul and heavy in the presence of a large crowd, and if the ventilation be insufficient, headache, dizziness, and death will ensue, as was the case in the terrible Black Hole of Calcutta. Unless you want to make a miniature "black hole" of your aquarium, do not overcrowd it. Let the water have light, but no sunshine. Put a glass cover over the tank to keep out the dust, but let the cover fit loosely enough to allow a free circulation of air. The glass top-piece will in a measure prevent evaporation. If, however, any water is lost from this cause, recollect that the salts contained in sea water do not evaporate, and consequently the tank may be replenished with fresh water equalling the amount evaporated. Beware of the hot summer months. I have always found it more difficult to keep the water pure during July and August than any other part of the year. Do not allow smoking in the room where your aquarium is, as the foul atmosphere taints the water. I once lost almost all the inhabitants of a thriving marine tank, by allowing a party of gentlemen to smoke in the room where it was standing. If you have company in the evening, the room, as a rule, will become overheated, and you should take the precaution to wrap the sides of the tank with wet towels.

The prepared food mentioned in the preceding chapter will answer for some salt-water animals. Lean beef, cut in very small bits, may be dried and kept for feeding marine pets when oysters or clams cannot be had. The clams and oysters should be chopped up very fine when used. Anemones and madrepores should be fed in quantities regulated by the size of the animals, and not more frequently than once a week. The food should be placed gently within their reach by means of a pair of forceps or some similar instrument. Crabs will soon learn to come out of their hiding-places at meal-times, and the fish will not be behind time in getting their share of chopped clam. If you have a vivarium (**FIGS. 21-4** and **21-5**), a handful of fiddler-crabs may be kept upon your artificial beach, where they will soon make themselves at home and afford a constant source of amusement by their antics. I kept a lot of little "fiddlers" in a fish globe, and for more than a year they lived without salt water, happy and contented with a bit of damp sand to dig in and an occasional piece

Fiddler Crabs

of chopped oyster to eat. It would be difficult to find odder or more easily satisfied pets than the grotesque little fiddlers. Each male crab has one large claw which for exercise or amusement he keeps in constant motion, only folding it up when preparing to enter his hole or scamper sideways across the sand. The pedunculated eyes of these little creatures stand up in a manner that gives them a very pert appearance.

Remove all dead animals or particles of food not devoured by the inmates, from the aquarium, to prevent the water from becoming tainted with poisonous gases emanating from the decaying animal matter. Dead vegetation, though not as injurious as dead animals, should nevertheless be removed, for it is unsightly, and makes the water turbid and muddy. No matter how foul sea-water may become, you must not waste it, for the injury is never permanent, and can soon be remedied by filtering or exposing it in earthenware vessels to the air and gently stirring it occasionally with a stick or piece of glass.

A filter may be made of a flower-pot, by stopping up the hole in the bottom with a perforated cork in which a small quill has been inserted, and then filling the pot half full of powdered charcoal, sand, and gravel—the charcoal at the bottom, the sand next, and the fine gravel or coarse sand on top. This filter when in use should be hung over, but some distance above, an earthen-ware dish, and the water allowed to fall drop by drop, or in a small stream, from the pot to the dish, or the filter may be hung over the aquarium, and each drop of water as it falls will carry with it into the tank below particles of the purifying, life-giving oxygen gathered up on its journey through the air.

CHAPTER 23

HOW TO COLLECT
FOR A MARINE
AQUARIUM

NEAR high-water mark, among the sea-weed and drift that have been washed up by a storm, is a veritable curiosity shop, and one well worth inspecting, but most of the animals to be found in this heterogeneous mass of drift, shells, plants, and pieces of wreck are either badly injured or dead, and, though many valuable specimens may here be obtained for the cabinet or museum, it is not a good place to find living, healthy animals for the aquarium.

If you are going on a collecting tour in search of living objects you must go prepared for a good rough-and-tumble time among slippery stones, muddy bottoms, or grimy old docks and piers.

You should wear no clothing that you care to preserve. Salt water will ruin shoes, so put on any old pair that will protect your feet from the shells or sharp stones; if the shoes have holes that let the water in, console yourself with the thought that the water can run out the same way. In fact, you must be prepared for a slip-up in the mud, or a good ducking in the shallow water, where the bottom is often so slippery that it is hard to wade far without involuntarily sitting down once or twice. After you have rigged yourself out in "old togs," next equip yourself with a basket to hold upright some glass preserve-jars or a lot of wide-mouthed bottles; then, armed with a small hammer, an old case-knife or trowel, a dip-net made of coarse bagging or fine mosquito-netting, you

The Young Collectors

are ready for any game from a lobster to the minute little crustacean found among the algæ.

You should time your excursion so as to be on the hunting-ground at extreme low tide. As soon as you reach the beach wade right into your work; look under the stones, scoop up the sand or mud with your net from the bottom of all the pools left by the tide, examine every promising-looking bunch of sea-weed, and before the tide comes in you will have material enough to stock forty aquariums. When you reach home sort out your specimens, discard all weak and sickly animals, and put the healthy ones in flat earthenware dishes of salt water, where they may be examined at leisure, and the proper ones taken out and put into your aquarium. In the mud and sand between the tides, or in the shallow water at extreme low tide, live many curious creatures.

If you should discover among the dirt in the bottom of your dip-net some queer-looking tubes, preserve them carefully, for they may contain some of those odd and often brilliantly colored marine worms. The inland boy, who is accustomed to see only the unsightly angle-worm, has no idea what really beautiful creatures some of the marine worms are. See, for instance, there is something in the mud that looks like a drop of blood. Put it in a plate of salt water and watch how one by one it begins to put forth its tentacles until its whole appearance is changed. This is a worm with a long scientific* name, which you may learn by and by if you become interested enough in your recreation to make a study of it.

Do not neglect to collect a few barnacles for your aquarium, and you will find yourself amply repaid for the trouble you found in detaching them from their native posts or rocks, when you see them each put forth an odd hand-shaped member, opening and closing the numerous long, slender fingers as if the animals inside the shells were grasping for something in the water, as, indeed, they are, for it is by this means that the little hermits in their acorn-shaped houses obtain their food.

For collecting in deep water, dredges are used; these are described in Chapter 9.

---

* Polycirrus eximius.

CHAPTER 24

DOGS

What They are Good For
and How to Train Them

It is true that a boy *can* do without a canine companion and live to enjoy life, but he is almost incomplete; he lacks something; he has lost a gratification, a harmless, pleasant experience, and the loss leaves an empty space in his boyhood life that nothing can ever quite fill up. A boy without a dog is like an unfinished story. What your left hand is to your right, a boy's dog is to the boy. More particularly is all this true of the lad who lives either in the country or within walking distance of forest and stream.

To be of any value either as a hunting dog, a watch dog or even a companion in one's rambles, it is absolutely necessary that the dog should be educated, and where there is a possibility of doing so, it is desirable to secure a young puppy. No matter what your choice in breed may be, whether it is a Newfoundland, bull, skye, greyhound, pointer, setter, or toy terrier, get the pup and *train it yourself.*

How to Choose a Dog

"Blood will tell," whether it flows in the veins of a horse, man, or dog. The reader can readily understand that it would be not only absurd but absolutely cruel to keep a Newfoundland, deer-hound, water-spaniel, pointer, setter, or any other similar breed of dog confined within the narrow limits of that small bit of ground attached to the city house and dignified by the name of a yard. It would be equally as absurd and almost as cruel for a farmer boy to try and keep one of those expensive, diminutive, delicate, nervous, city dogs known under the general title of a "toy dog" or "fancy breed." The agile, bright-eyed "black-and-tan," and the delicate and graceful Italian greyhound, are full of fun, but as unreliable as beautiful. Thoughtless, rollicking, exquisites! Such dogs are scarcely the kind either city or country boy would choose for playmates or companions. What most boys want is a dog that combines the qualities of a boon companion and a good watch dog. By the latter is meant a dog whose intelligence is sufficient for it to discriminate between friend and foe, and whose courage will prompt it to attack the latter without hesitancy. It must also be a dog that may be taught to "fetch" and carry, to hunt for rat, squirrel, or rabbit, as well as to obey and trust in its master. It should be so cleanly in his habits as to be unobjectionable in-doors, and should possess judgment enough to know when its company is not agreeable, and at such times keep out of the way.

The poodle is perhaps the best trick dog, but is disliked by many on account of its thick woolly coat being so difficult to keep clean. The wirey-haired Scotch terrier is a comical, intelligent animal, and a first-rate comrade for a boy. The Newfoundland is faithful, companionable, and powerful enough to protect children, to whom, if there be any around the house, it will become very much attached and a self-constituted guardian. The spaniel is pretty, affectionate, and docile.

Almost all the sporting dogs make first-class watch-dogs, but are restless and troublesome if confined, and, as a rule, they are too large for the house. The shepherd is remarkably intelligent, and, when well trained, makes a trusty dog for general purposes.

The bull, although not necessarily as fierce and vicious as one would suppose from its looks and reputation, still is hardly the dog for a pet or companion, being of a dull and heavy nature, and not lively enough to suit the taste of the boy of the period. A little of the bull mixed in the blood of another more lively breed makes a good dog, of which a thorough-bred bull-terrier is an example. The Rev. J. G. Wood, in speaking of the latter, says:

"The skilful dog-fancier contrives a judicious mixture of the two breeds, and engrafts the tenacity, endurance, and dauntless courage of the bull-dog upon the more agile and frivolous terrier. Thus he obtains a dog that can do almost anything, and though, perhaps, it may not surpass, it certainly rivals almost every other variety of dog in its accomplishments. In the capacity for learning tricks it scarcely yields, if it does yield at all, to the poodle. It can retrieve as well as the dog which is especially bred for that purpose. It can hunt the fox with the regular hounds, it can swim and dive as well as the Newfoundland dog. In the house it is one of the wariest and most intelligent of dogs, permitting no unaccustomed footstep to enter 'the domains without giving warning.'" Although some may think the Rev. J. G. Wood to be a little too enthusiastic in his description of the bull-terrier's good qualities, still if they have ever owned a properly trained animal of this breed, they will undoubtedly agree with the great naturalist so far as to acknowledge this particular dog to be about the best for a boy's dog. With an ardor not excelled by his young master, the bull-terrier will chase any sort of game, and will attack and fight any foe at its master's bidding. Indeed the great fault of this kind of dog is that it is inclined to be too quarrelsome among other dogs, and careful attention should be paid to correcting this fault, which may be entirely eradicated by kind and firm treatment; but should any canine bully attack your pet, woe be unto him, for, unless he comes from good fighting stock, he will rue the day he ever picked that quarrel.

How to Train Dogs

First of all teach your dog that you mean *exactly what you say*, and that he *must* obey you. To do this you should never give a foolish command;

but if a thoughtless order be once given, even though you repent it as soon as it has escaped from your lips, do not hesitate, but insist upon your pupil instantly obeying—that is, if the dog, in your judgment, understands the order. Never, under any circumstances, allow him to shirk, and even a naturally stupid pup will learn to look upon your word as law and not think of disobeying.

Strict obedience to your word, whistle or slightest gesture once obtained, it is an easy task to finish the dog's education. Bear in mind that there is about as great a difference in the character and natural intelligence of dogs as there is in boys. Not only does this exist between the distinct varieties of dogs, but also between the different individuals of the same variety. All Newfoundlands possess similar characteristics, but each individual varies considerably in intelligence, amiability, and all those little traits that go to make up a dog's character. I mention this fact that you may not be disappointed, or make your poor dog suffer because it cannot learn as fast or as much as some one you may know of. And here let me say, and impress upon your mind, that to make your dog obey, or to teach it the most difficult trick or feat, it is seldom necessary to use the whip. If the dog, as he sometimes will do, knowingly and wilfully disobeys, the whip may be used sparingly; one sharp blow is generally sufficient; it should be accompanied with a reprimand in words. Never lose your patience and beat an animal in anger. To successfully train a dog it is necessary to place the greatest restraint upon your own feelings, for if you once give way to anger the dog will know it, and one-half your influence is gone. To be sure the special line of education depends upon the kind of a dog you have, and what you want him to do.

The pointer or setter you may commence to teach to "stand," at a very early age, using first a piece of meat, praising and petting him when he does well, and reprimanding when required. Do not tire your pup out, but if he does well once let him play and sleep before trying again. As he grows older, replace the meat with a dead bird. The best sportsmen of today do not allow their bird dogs to retrieve, saying that the "mouthing" of the dead and bloody birds affects the fineness of their noses. To bring in birds, the sportsman has following at his heels a cocker spaniel, large poodle, or almost any kind of dog, who is taught to follow patiently and obediently until game is killed and he receives the order to "fetch."

To Teach a Dog to Retrieve

Commence with the young pup. Almost any dog will chase a ball and very soon learn to bring it to his master. When you have taught your dog to "fetch," he may be tried with game. It is very probable that the first bird he brings will be badly "mouthed;" that is, bitten and mangled; to break him of this, prepare a ball of yarn so wound over pins that the slightest pressure will cause the points to protrude and prick any object pressed against the ball. After the dog has pricked his mouth once or twice with this ball he will learn to pick it up and carry it in the most delicate manner; he may then be tried again with a bird. This time he will probably bring it to you without so much as ruffling a feather; but if notwithstanding his experience with a ball of pins your dog still "mouths" the game, you must skin a bird and arrange the ball and pins inside the bird skin so as to prick sharply upon a light pressure; make the dog "fetch" the bird skin until he is completely broken of his bad habit of biting or "mouthing" game.

Pointers and Setters

At first you will have to give your commands by word of mouth, but if you accompany each command by an appropriate gesture, the pup will soon learn to understand and obey the slightest motion of the hand or head. The less noise there is the greater is the chance of killing game. Nothing is more un-sportsmanlike than shouting in a loud voice to your dog while in the field.

After teaching a dog to "heel," "down charge," and to "hi on" at command, you may show him game and teach him to "quarter" his ground by moving yourself in the direction you wish the dog to go. The dog will not be long in understanding and obeying.

When your pointer comes to a point teach him to be steady by repeating softly, "steady, boy, steady," at the same time holding up your hand. In course of time the words may be omitted; the hand raised as a caution will keep the dog steady; but should he break point and flush the game, as a young dog is more than liable to do, you may give him the whip and at the same time use some appropriate words that the dog will remember; the next time the word without the whip will correct him. After your dog has been taught to obey, it is well to put him in the field with an old, well-trained dog.

As every sportsman has a peculiar system of his own for breaking a dog, it is scarcely necessary for me to give more than these few hints; only let me again caution you against using the whip too often. Spare the lash and keep a good stock of patience on hand; otherwise in breaking the dog you will also break his spirit and have a mean, treacherous animal that will slink and cringe at your slightest look, but seldom obey you when he thinks he is out of reach of the dreaded whip.

Pet Dogs

All dogs, whether intended for the field, for pets, or for companions, should be taught to follow at their master's heels at the command of "heel," to run ahead at the command of "hi on," and to drop at the command of "charge" or "down charge." When your dog learns to obey these simple commands, it will be found an easy matter to extricate and keep your canine friend out of scrapes. Suppose you have a small but pugnacious dog and in your walk you meet a large, ugly-tempered brute much too powerful for your own dog to master in the fight that is certain to ensue unless by some command you can prevent it. The strange dog will not obey you, but if you give the order to "heel" to your own dog he will follow with his nose at your heels, and the enemy will seldom if ever attack a dog while so near his master.

Study the characteristics of your dog, and by taking advantage of its peculiarities it may be taught many amusing tricks. I have a little dog called Monad, and whether his master walks, drives, sails or rows Monad always accompanies him, even sitting in front of the sliding seat of a single shell boat for hours at a time, perfectly happy and apparently conscious of the attention he attracts from all people on the shore or in the passing boats; the latter he generally salutes with a bark. Monad will, when requested to do so, close a door, sneeze, bark, or sit upon his haunches and rub his nose, besides numerous other amusing tricks.

One day Monad smelled of a lighted cigar; the smoke inhaled caused him to sneeze; this gave me an idea; lighting a match I held it toward him, at the same time repeating, "sneeze! sneeze, sir!" The smoke made him sneeze, and after repeating the operation several times I held out an unlighted match and commanded him to sneeze; the dog sneezed at once. It was then an easy step to make him sneeze at the word without the match. Monad is now very proud of this accomplishment, and when desirous of "showing off" always commences by sneezing.

In much the same manner I taught him to rub his nose by blowing in his face and repeating the words, "rub your nose." The breath coming in contact with that sensitive organ apparently tickled it and he would rub it with his paws. After one or two trials he learned to rub his little black nose in a very comical manner whenever commanded to do so. By patting your leg with your hand and at the same time calling your dog, it will learn to come to you and place his fore paws against your leg. If you take advantage of this and pat the door the next time with your hand, the dog will stand on its hind legs and rest its fore paws against the door. Reward him with a bit of meat or a caress, and then opening the door a few inches go through with the same performance, giving the command to close the door; by degrees, as the dog learns, open the door wider, and without moving from your chair or position in the room give the command, "close the door, sir." The dog will by this time understand your meaning, and resting his fore paws against the panels, follow the door until it closes with a bang. Perhaps there is no simple trick that excites more surprise than this. A friend comes in and leaves the door open; you rise, greet your friend, ask him to be seated; then, as if for the first time noticing the fact of the door being open, speak to your dog; the latter closes the door and lies down again by the fireside in a most methodical manner. The friend is thoroughly convinced that that particular dog has more sense than any other canine in the world, and ever after, when dogs are the topic of conversation, he will tell the story of the dog that shut the door.

In the same manner innumerable odd, amusing, or useful tricks may be taught, among the simplest of which are the ones which excite the most applause from spectators. If your dog is fond of carrying a stick in his mouth, it will be an easy matter to make him carry a basket. Take advantage of every peculiarity of your pet's character, encouraging and developing the good points, but keeping the bad traits subdued, and you will soon have an amusing and reasoning canine companion.

Never throw a dog into the water; it frightens him and makes the poor animal dread a bath. Let the dog wade at first; then by throwing sticks or other objects a little further out each time, and commanding him to fetch, the dog will not only learn to swim after the object, but also learn to thoroughly enjoy the bath, and can even be taught to dive and jump off of high places. There are dogs that will jump from an elevation twelve feet above the water. Always be firm but kind; teach your dog to have confidence in you, and you may place implicit trust in your canine friend, and be sure whatever misfortune befalls you, you will have a friend who, though he be a four-footed one, will never forsake you, but live and die for the master it has learned to love and trust.

CHAPTER 25

INSECTS

Preserving Insects

Great care must be taken in killing insects, intended for the cabinet, and death should be produced without disfiguring them or rubbing off the down or scales that covers the bodies and wings of some specimens. A convenient and successful way to kill insects is to drop them into a wide-mouthed bottle, the bottom of which is lined with blotting-paper that has been previously saturated with ether, benzine, creosote or chloroform. When a butterfly, bug, or beetle is put into a bottle prepared in this manner, and the bottle tightly corked, the insect expires without a struggle, and hence without injuring itself. From the bottle the specimens may be taken and pinned upon a mounting-board, consisting of two strips of wood resting upon supports at each end, a space being left between the strips for the body of the insect. Under this space or crack a piece of cork is fastened (**FIG. 25-1**) in which to stick the point of the pin. After pinning the specimen to the mounting-board, spread the wings and legs out in a natural position, and if it be a butterfly or moth, fasten its wings in position with bits of paper

FIG. 25-1

Top View, End View and Mounting-Board

231

Butterfly pinned to Mounting-Board

Beetle, with legs set and Leg-pin

Cross Section of Morse Insect Box

and pins, as shown in **FIG. 25-2**. An ingenious and simple device for pinning the leg of an insect is illustrated by **FIG. 25-3**. It consists of two needles with their heads driven into a small pine stick.

Morse Insect Box

Mr. E. S. Morse gives probably the best device for arranging an insect box for the cabinet. It consists of a light wooden frame with paper stretched upon the upper and under surface. Dampen the paper and glue it to the frame; when the paper dries it will contract and become as tight as a drum-head. Inside the box upon two sides fasten cleats, and let their top edges be about one-quarter of an inch above the bottom. Rest the paper-covered frame upon these cleats and secure it in position. The bottom of the box should be lined with soft pine to receive the point of the pins. The space under the frame can be dusted with snuff and camphor to keep out such insects as delight to feed upon the prepared specimens of their relatives. **FIG. 25-4** shows a cross section of a box upon Mr. Morse's plan.

The Lawrence Breeding Box

The best moths and butterflies are obtained by rearing the caterpillars in cages made for the purpose. I am indebted to Mr. Albert Lawrence for the accompanying plan of a larvae box, invented and used by himself for several seasons (see **FIG.**

FIG. 25-5

*Mr. Albert Lawrence's
Breeding Box*

25-5). The Lawrence box, as may be seen by the diagram, can be taken apart and packed away when not in use or during transportation.

The sides, ends, and top are wooden frames covered with wire netting; the bottom is a flat board. They are all joined by hook and screweyes. To take them apart it is necessary to unfasten the hooks.

Spiders

are very likely to lose their colors if placed in spirits, and if pinned and dried like beetles they will not only lose all color, but their bodies will shrivel up and change in form and proportion to such a degree as to make the specimens next to worthless. Mr. Ralph Hemingray, of Covington, Ky., sent the author some spider bottles manufactured under his direction of very thick, clear, white glass, three inches high by one and one-quarter inch broad, and three-quarters of an inch thick.

FIG. 25-6

The Hemingray Bottle

These bottles are convenient in shape, and when a spider is put in one and the bottle filled with glycerine, the spider looks as if it might be imbedded in a solid block of crystal.

I have had some brightly colored garden spiders preserved in this manner for two years, and they have not only retained their original shape but color also. In the place of corks, pieces of elastic are stretched over the tops of the bottles; this allows the glycerine to expand or contract. **FIG. 25-6** represents a drawing of one of these bottles with a spider in it. A case of specimens preserved in this manner makes not only an interesting cabinet, but a very pretty one. Although many persons have a horror of spiders, they lose all their nervousness when the insects are seen neatly labelled and enclosed in pretty glass bottles.

How to Make Beautiful or Comical Groups and Designs of Insects

Many really beautiful, as well as some absurdly comical designs can be made of properly preserved insects by ingenious lads.

Butterflies may be made to have the appearance of hovering in mid-air by mounting them upon extremely fine wire.

Grasshoppers can be arranged in comical, human-like attitudes.

Beetles may be harnessed like horses to a tiny car made of the half of an English walnut-shell. A very pretty design can be made by seating a grasshopper in a delicate sea-shell of some kind, and glueing the shell to a bit of looking-glass; fine wires attached to the shell will answer the double purpose of a support and harness for a couple of flying beetles; a little moss glued around the sides so as to conceal the ragged edges of the glass will add greatly to the effect, and the whole will have the appearance of a fairy boat being drawn over the surface of the water by two flying beetles, guided by the long-legged imp in the shell.

Preserved insects are exceedingly brittle, the least touch will often break off a wing or leg or otherwise disfigure the specimen, hence it is necessary not only to be very careful in handling them, but to supply some sort of cover to protect them from accidents, dust, and injurious insects. Dome-shape glass-covers are best adapted for small groups or compositions, and these may be obtained from the dealers at moderate prices, or, if the young taxidermist has acquired sufficient skill to make his work valuable, he can readily trade off duplicate specimens for glass-covers, as many amateurs as well as some professionals do.

PART VI
THE BOY GAMER

CHAPTER 26

KITE TIME

IT is a pleasant sensation to sit in the first spring sunshine and feel the steady pull of a good kite upon the string, and watch its graceful movements as it sways from side to side, ever mounting higher and higher, as if impatient to free itself and soar away amid the clouds. The pleasure is, however, greatly enhanced by the knowledge that the object skimming so bird-like and beautifully through the air is a kite of your own manufacture.

I remember, when quite a small boy, building an immense man kite, seven feet high. It was a gorgeous affair, with its brilliant red nose and cheeks, blue coat, and striped trousers.

As you may imagine, I was nervous with anxiety and excitement to see it fly. After several experimental trials to get the tail rightly balanced, and the breast-band properly adjusted, and having procured the strongest hempen twine with which to fly it, I went to the river-bank for the grand event.

My man flew splendidly; he required no running, no hoisting, no jerking of the string to assist him. I had only to stand on the high bank and let out the string, and so fast did the twine pass through my hands that my fingers were almost blistered. People began to stop and gaze at the queer sight, as my man rose higher and higher, when, suddenly, my intense pride and enjoyment was changed into something very like fright.

The twine was nearly all paid out, when I found that my man was stronger than his master, and I could not hold him! Imagine, if you can, my dismay. I fancied myself being pulled from the bank into the river, and skimming through the water at lightning speed, for, even in my fright, the idea of letting go of the string did not once occur to me. However, to my great relief, a man standing near came to my assistance, just as the stick upon which the twine had been wound came dancing up from the ground toward my hands. So hard did my giant pull that even the friend who had kindly come to the rescue had considerable trouble to hold him in. The great kite, as it swung majestically about, high in the blue sky, attracted quite a crowd of spectators, and I felt very grand at the success of my newly invented flying-man; but my triumph was short-lived. The tail made of rags was too heavy to bear its own weight, and, breaking off near the kite, it fell to the ground, while my kite, freed from this load, shot up like a rocket, then turned and came headlong down with such force, that dashing through the branches of a thorny locust-tree, it crashed to the ground, a mass of broken sticks and tattered paper. Although the sad fate of my first man-kite taught me to avoid building unmanageable giants, the experiment was, on the whole, satisfactory, for it proved beyond a doubt that it is unnecessary to follow the conventional form for a kite to make one that will fly.

Man Kite

To make this kite you will require four sticks, some rattan and some paper. In regard to his size, I would suggest that the larger the man is, the better he will fly. Now let us suppose you are going to make this fellow four feet high. First, cut two straight sticks three feet nine inches long; these are to serve for the legs and body; cut another straight stick two and one-half feet in length for the spine, and a fourth stick, three feet five inches long, for the arms. For the head select a light piece of split rattan—any light, tough wood that will bend readily will do—bend this in a circle eight inches in diameter, fasten it securely to one end of the spine by binding it with strong thread, being careful that the spine runs exactly through the centre of the circle (**FIG. 26-2**). Next find the exact centre of the arm-stick, and with a pin or small tack fasten it at this point to the spine, a few inches below the chin (**FIG. 26-3**). After wrapping the joint tightly with strong thread, lay the part of the skeleton which is finished flat upon the floor, mark two points upon the arm-sticks for the shoulder-joints, each seven inches from the intersection of the spine and arm-stick, which will place them fourteen inches apart. At these points fasten with a pin the two long sticks that are reserved for the body and legs (**FIG. 26-4**). Now cross these sticks as shown in diagram, being careful that the terminations of the lower limbs are at least three feet apart; the waist-joint ought then to be about ten inches below the arm-stick. After taking the greatest pains to see that the arm-stick is perfectly at right angles with the spine, fasten all the joints securely. Upon the arms bind oblong loops of rattan, or of the same material as the head-frame. These hand-loops ought to be about three inches broad at their widest parts, and exact counterparts of each other. The loops for the feet must

FIG. 26-2

FIG. 26-3

FIG. 26-4

approach as nearly as possible the shape of feet, and these, too, must be exactly alike, or the kite will be "lopsided," or unequally balanced. Now cut two sticks three inches long for the ends of sleeves, and two others four inches long for bottoms of trousers (**FIG. 26-5**); fasten the two former near the ends of the arm-stick, and the two latter near the ends of the leg-sticks, as in the illustration. The strings of the frame must next be put on, as shown by the dotted lines (**FIG. 26-6**). Commence with the neck, at equal distances from the spine, and about seven

FIG. 26-5

FIG. 26-6

Frame of Man Kite

inches apart; tie two strings to the arm-sticks; extend these strings slantingly to the head, and fasten them to the hoop, one on each side of the spine, and about five inches apart. Take another thread and fasten to the top of cross-stick of right arm, pass it over and take a wrap around the spine, continue it to top of cross-stick upon left arm, and there tie it. Fasten another string to bottom of cross-stick on right arm, draw it tight and wrap it on spine four inches below intersection of arm-stick, pass it on to the bottom of cross-stick on left arm, draw taut and fasten it. Tie the body-string at the right shoulder-joint, drop the thread down to a point exactly opposite the termination of spine upon the right leg, take a wrap, and draw the line across to point upon left leg exactly opposite, bind it there, then bring it up to left shoulder-joint and tie it. For the trousers fasten a string at a point on right arm-stick, eleven inches from the intersection of spine, extend it down in a straight line to inside end of cross-stick of left limb and fasten it there. Tie another string at a point one inch and a half to the left of spine upon right arm-stick, extend it down in a straight line to outside end of cross-stick of left limb. Go through the same process for right leg of trousers, and the frame-work will be complete.

For the covering of a kite of this size I have always used tissue paper; it is pretty in color and very light in weight. Paste some sheets of tissue paper together, red for the trousers, hands and face, blue for the coat, and black, or some dark color, for the feet. Use paste made of flour and water boiled to the consistency of starch. Put the paste on with a small bristle brush, make the seams or over-laps hardly more than one-fourth of an inch wide, and press them together with a soft rag or towel; measure the paper so that the coat will join the trousers at the proper place. When you are satisfied that this is all right, lay the paper smoothly on the floor and place the frame of the kite upon it, using heavy books or paper-weights to hold it in place. Then with a pair of scissors cut the paper around the frame, leaving a clear edge of one-half inch, and making a slit in this margin or edge every six or seven inches and at each angle; around the head these slits must be made about two or three inches apart to prevent the paper from wrinkling when you commence to paste. With your brush cover the margin with paste one section at a time, turn them over, and with the towel or rag press them down. After the kite is all pasted and dry, take a large paint-brush, and with black marking-paint, india ink, or common writing fluid, put in the buttons and binding on coat with a good broad touch. The face and hair must be painted with broad lines, so that they may be seen clearly at a great height. Follow this rule wherever you have to use paint upon any kind of kite.

The breast-band, or "belly-band," of the man kite should be arranged in the same manner as it is upon the common hexagonal or coffin-shaped kite with which all American boys are familiar; but for fear some of my readers may not quite understand I will try and tell them exactly how to do it. First, punch small holes through the paper, one upon each side of the leg-sticks just above the bottom of the pants, and one upon each side of the arm-stick at the shoulders. Run one end of the breast-band through the holes at the bottom of the left limb and tie it fast to the leg-stick; tie the other end at the right shoulder. Take another string of the same length as the first and fasten one end in the same manner at the bottom of the right leg, pass the string up, crossing the first band, and tie the end at the left shoulder. Attach your kite-string to the breast-band where the two strings intersect in such a manner that you can slide the kite-string up or down until it is properly adjusted. For the tail-band, tie a string (to the leg-sticks) at the bottom of the breast-band and let it hang slack from one leg to the other. Attach the tail to the centre of this string. By a slight modification of the frame of the man kite you can produce:

FIG. 26-7

Frame of Boy Kite

FIG. 26-8

The Boy Kite

FIG. 26-9

Frame of Frog Kite

A Boy Kite

that will create an unlimited amount of fun whenever he makes his appearance in his aesthetic Kate Greenaway suit. By carefully following the construction according to the diagram (**FIG. 26-7**) the average boy will find little difficulty in building a twin brother to the kite in the illustration (**FIG. 26-8**).

Still another strange looking kite can be made by using a piece of pliable wood bent in a circular form for the body, and allowing the leg-sticks to protrude above the shoulders to form short arms, the spine extending below the trunk some distance to form the tail to a

Frog Kite

It is not worth while to build one less than two feet high. Let us suppose that the particular batrachian we are now about to make is to be just that height; in this case the leg-sticks must be each two feet long, and as you will want to bend them at the knees, these points should be made considerably thinner than the other parts of the sticks. The spine must be about one foot seven inches long, or a little over three-quarters of the length of the leg-sticks. Place the two latter one above the other, lay the spine on top of them, and see that the tops of all three are flush, or perfectly even. Then at a point eight inches from the top, drive a pin through all three sticks, carefully clamping it upon the other side where the point protrudes. For the body, take a piece of thin rattan two feet five or six inches in length, bend it into the form of a circle, allowing the ends to overlap an inch or two that they may be firmly bound together with thread by winding it around the joint. The circle will be about eight inches in diameter. Take the three sticks you pinned together and lay them on the floor, spreading them apart in the form of an irregular star, in such a manner that the top of the spine will be just half-way between the tops of the leg-sticks and about five inches from each; when you have proceeded thus far place the rattan circle over the other sticks; the intersection of the sticks should be the centre of the circle; with pins and thread fasten the frame together in this position. The lower limbs will be spread wide apart; they must be carefully drawn closer together and held in position by a string tied near the termination of each leg-stick. Cross-sticks for hands and feet may now be added, and the strings put on as shown in **FIG. 26-9**. This kite should be covered with green tissue paper. A few marks of the paint-brush will give it the appearance of **FIG. 26-10**. The breast and tail-band can be put on as described in the man kite.

FIG. 26-10

Frog Kite

The Butterfly Kite

Make a thin straight stick of a piece of elastic wood, or split rattan; to the top end of this attach a piece of thread or string; bend the stick as you would a bow until it forms an arc or part of a circle; then holding the stick in this position tie the other end of the string to a point a few inches above the bottom end of the stick. At a point on the stick, about one-quarter the distance from the top, tie another string, draw it taut, and fasten it to the bottom end of the bow. Take another stick of exactly the same length and thickness as the first, and go through the same process, making a frame that must be a duplicate of the other. Then fasten the two frames together, as shown by **FIG. 26-11**, allowing the arcs to overlap several inches, and bind the joints securely with thread.

FIG. 26-11

Frame of Butterfly Kite

FIG. 26-12

The Butterfly Kite

The head of the insect is made by attaching two broom-straws to the top part of the wings where they join, the straws must be crossed, the projecting ends serving for the antennæ or, as the boys call them, the "smellers" of the butterfly. Now select a piece of yellow or blue tissue paper, place your frame over it, cut and paste as directed in the description of the man kite. When the kite is dry, with black paint make some marking upon the wings similar to those shown in the illustration, **FIG. 26-12**; or, better still, cut out some pieces of dark colored paper in the form of these markings and paste them on, of course taking care to have one wing like the other (**FIG. 26-12**), as in nature.

The King Crab Kite

The king, or "horse shoe crab," is familiar to all boys who live upon the coast or spend their summer vacation at the sea-side. It is a comparatively simple matter to imitate this crustacean in the form of a kite; in fact, all that is necessary is a slight modification of the old-fashioned bow kite to which a pointed tail must be attached. This tail can be made as shown in the illustration (**FIG. 26-13**), or may be cut out of a piece of paste-board and joined to the kite by a paper hinge; this will allow the tail to bend backward when the wind blows against it, giving it a natural appearance; the kite and pointed tail, which is part of the kite, should be covered with yellow paper. If you think that you do not possess sufficient skill with the brush to represent the under side of the crab, as shown in the illustration (**FIG. 26-14**), you can, at least, paint two large eyespots some distance apart near the upper end, and then your kite will represent a back view. Attach the breast and tail bands as on an ordinary bow kite.

Fish Kite

Cut two straight pine sticks; shave them down until they are thin enough to bend readily; see that they are exactly the same length and

FIG. 26-13

Frame of King Crab

FIG. 26-14

King Crab Kite

of about the same weight. Fasten the top ends together by driving a pin through them. Bend each stick in the form of a bow, and hold them in this position until you have secured a third stick across them at right angles about one-third the way down from the top, or ends where they are joined together. The fish should be about half as broad as it is long. Let the lower ends of the side or bow sticks cross each other far enough up to form a tail to the fish, and fasten the sticks together at their intersection. Before stringing the frame see that the cross-stick protrudes an equal distance from each side of the fish. To make the tail, tie a string across the bottom from the end of one cross-stick to the end of the other, and to this string midway between the two side-sticks tie another string, pass it up to the root of the tail, draw it taut and fasten it there at the intersection of the side-sticks, this will make a natural hooking-fork to the caudal fin (**FIG. 26-15**).

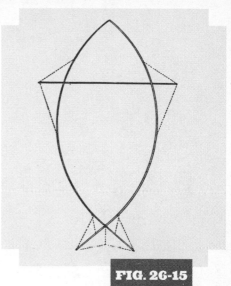

FIG. 26-15

Frame of Fish Kite

The remainder of the strings can be put on by referring to the diagram, care being taken that the dorsal or back-fin is made exactly the same size as the fin on the belly of the fish. Yellow, red, and green are all appropriate colors for the paper covering of this kite. After the paper is pasted and dry you may amuse yourself by painting the outlines of the gills and fins (**FIG. 26-16**). The kite will look all the better for not having the scales painted upon it. Tie the strings of the breast-band to the side-sticks near the head and tail, and let them cross each other as in a common kite. Attach the tail-band to the tail of the fish.

FIG. 26-16

Fish Kite

The Turtle Kite

is so simple in its construction that a lengthy description of how to make it would be out of place. All that is necessary is to place the

FIG. 26-17

Frame of Turtle Kite

FIG. 26-18

The Turtle Kite

FIG. 26-19

Frame of Shield Kite

diagram before you (**FIG. 26-17**) and go to work. Suppose you want your kite to measure two feet from tip of nose to end of tail, the spine or centre-stick must then, of course, be two feet long; make the leg-sticks each one and a half foot long, place the stick for the fore-legs at a point on the spine seven inches below the top, put the stick for the hind-legs eight inches below the fore-legs. Adjust the hoop so that it will extend four inches above the fore-leg stick and the same distance below the hind-leg stick. Let the diameter across the centre from side to side be about fifteen inches. Put the crosspieces on for the head and feet, run a thread over the bottom end of the spine for a tail, cover the whole with green tissue paper and your kite is done (**FIG. 26-18**).

The Shield Kite

Make the frame of four sticks, two straight cross-sticks and two bent side-sticks (**FIG. 26-19**); cover it with red, white, and blue tissue paper. Paste red and white paper together in stripes for the bottom, and use a blue ground with white stars for the top (**FIG. 26-20**). The next kite is not original with the author, but is well known in some sections of the country. I have made a diagram of it at the request of a number of boys who did not know how to make

A Star Kite

Build it according to the diagrams (**FIGS. 26-21** and **26-22**), making the sticks all of equal length, and cover the kite with any colored paper that may suit your fancy.

The Chinese Dragon Kite

This kite is a most resplendent affair, and glitters in the sunlight as if it were covered with jewels. It is rather complicated to look at, but not very difficult to make. The one I have before me was made in China.

The top or horizontal stick (**FIG. 26-23, 1-2**) is three feet long, half an inch wide, and one-eighth inch thick. The face can be simplified by using a loop, as in the man kite. Two more loops, as shown in the diagram, will serve as frames for the wings. Paper is pasted upon this, and hangs loose like an apron in front below the cross-stick (**FIGURE 26-23, 1-2**). Cut the paper long enough to cover the first disk of the tail-piece, as shown in the finished kite, **FIG. 26-26**. The head-piece is ornamented with brilliant colors, bits of looking-glass pasted on or attached with strings, so that they dangle loosely, etc.; this makes the top rather heavy, as, in fact, it ought to be, for then it serves to balance the tail, which, in this instance, is a succession of circular kites, ten inches in diameter, and thirteen in number, connected with one another by strings. Attached to each of these paper disks is a slender piece of reed or grass with a tufted head; a similar tuft is fastened by a string to the opposite end to balance it. The breast-band is made like that upon an ordinary kite; the cross-strings, being attached to the face at the top and bottom, intersect each other about opposite a point between the eyes.

FIG. 26-24 represents the top view of a single disk, showing where the reeds and string are attached. **FIG. 26-25** shows a side view of two disks, and the way in which they are connected by strings, six and a half inches space being left between each two disks. A (**FIG. 26-26**) is a front view of finished kite.

FIG. 26-20

The Shield Kite

FIG. 26-21

Frame of Star Kite

FIG. 26-22

Star Kite

FIG. 26-23

FIG. 26-24

FIG. 26-25

*Portion of
Framework of Tail*

The Japanese Square Kite

is not, as its name might imply, perfectly square. It is rectangular in form, and made with a framework of very thin bamboo or cane sticks, bound together as shown in **FIG. 26-27**. This frame is covered with Japanese paper, to which all the sticks are tightly glued. The kite is bent backward, making the front slightly convex, and held in this position by strings tied from end to end of the cross-sticks at the back; the breast-band may be attached as on an ordinary six-sided kite. Instead of a tail-band, with a single tail attached, this foreigner carries two tails, one tied at each side to the protruding ends of the diagonal sticks at the bottom of the kite. The illustration on page 240, of two boys making ready to fly one of these kites, is a copy from a picture made by a Japanese artist.

The Moving Star

is a paper lantern attached to the tail of any large kite.

A Chinese lantern will answer this purpose, although it is generally so long and narrow that the motion of the kite is apt to set fire to it.

To make a more suitable lantern, take a circular piece of light board five inches in diameter, drive three nails in the centre just far enough apart to allow a candle to fit between them firmly. Make of rattan or wire a light hoop of the same diameter as the bottom-piece; fasten these to a strap or handle of wood, or wire, as shown in the diagram (**FIG. 26-28**), and cover the body of the lantern with red tissue paper.

This lantern fastened to the tail of a large kite that is sent up on a dark night will go bobbing around in a most eccentric and apparently unaccountable manner, striking with wonder all observers not in the secret.

Biggest Kite on Record

On September 27, 1885, The United Kite-Raising Association, of Yorkville, attempted to send up the biggest kite on record. The cloth that covered it weighted fourteen pounds, and the kite was sixteen feet high and fourteen feet wide, with a tail four hundred feet long.

The wind was too light to keep the monster up, but the crowd had "lots of fun" in the attempt.

In New York City there is a law, passed in the interest of the telegraph companies, which imposes a fine of five dollars on any one raising a kite south of Fourteenth Street; but since the law was passed, the boys have had ample revenge in seeing the telegraph poles condemned as a public nuisance, and cut down.

It does not appear that "Section 249 of the Corporation Ordinance," as the kite law is termed, is known to the boys, or enforced by the police, as the following item, clipped from one of the New York newspapers, will plainly demonstrate:

FIG. 26-26

The Chinese Dragon Kite

Thousand Of Kites

The Curious Fleet Of Air Craft Which
Hovers Over The East Side

Anybody riding up the Second Avenue railway on a fine breezy afternoon will become impressed with the belief that kite-flying must be one of the leading East Side industries. The air fairly swarms with kites. They hover like a great flock of birds over all that section of the city east of the Bowery between Chatham Square and the Cooper Institute. There are kites of all descriptions, from the big, majestic, "six-cornered" kind that hang motionless save now and then a grave nod and a languid swing of the long tail to the fierce little rattle-headed Chinese variety that take the form of great butterflies and beetles, and dart hither and thither without a moment's rest. When the

FIG. 26-27

Japanese Square Kite Frame

sunlight falls right, a faint, shadowy maze of strings can be seen running from the kites to countless house roofs. It is not always small boys who are attached to the kites by the strings. Idle, hulking fellows, old enough to be at something better, loll away afternoons lazily watching their kites drift away as they feed them out string. As for the telegraph, telephone, and electric light wires along these streets, they are so hung with kite wrecks and festooned with bedraggled kite tails that they look like lines hung with the washing of a rag fair.

Last Saturday was a great day for kites. Thousands of them flecked the sky over the East Side, and only one was above the Fourteenth Street. But that was purely accidental. It was flown from a roof within the forbidden territory.

New York City boys, as a rule, have very little practical knowledge of the manner of making kites, but depend upon the shops for their supply. There is a portly German on Prince Street who for twenty years has supplied the small boys of New York City with their kites, and he says that kite time does not begin here before the Fourth of July.

Since the first edition of the "American Boy's Handy Book" appeared, but one suggestion on a new form of kite has been received; and, as the author subsequently saw one of the kites fly successfully, he takes pleasure in quoting the letter, and in adding to the list in the book:

The Tailless Kite—Holland Kite

Rochester, New York, January 6, 1882. Friend Elwood: In "The American Boy's Handy Book," a copy of which you presented to my son Christmas last, I do not see that easily-made and always-successful, tailless Holland kite, a great number of which I have made for my own and other boys.

The draft represents a kite four feet long. The proportions must be mathematically correct. Stick (B, F **FIG. 26-29**) four feet long; the cross-stick (C, D **FIG. 26-29**) is a bow, made of ash, hickory, oak, or split reed, just three feet long, with strings attached to each end and tied at the back, to give it the proper curve. This curve must be varied with the strength of the wind. If the wind is strong, tighten the bow-cord, and give it more curve. The bow and stick are fastened to each other one foot from upper end of the stick and at A, **FIG. 26-30**, the centre of the bow.

FIG. 26-30

Attach belly-band at contact of stick and bow (A), and at lower end of stick (B); and to determine the length of belly-band, let its angle just reach end of bow, C or D, at which angle the kite-string is to be attached.

These kites may be made of any size, but these proportions must be strictly observed. Each side must be equal in weight. Lift the kite by belly-string, balancing lower end on a finger pivot, and if it tips to one side, paste pieces of paper to the light side, till they are equal. The stick and bow must be as light as their duties will warrant.

These kites require no tails. Just the right weight and length for an old style kite tail has never been determined, and this uncertainty caused much unhappiness with the boys of my time.

The first of these tailless kites that I made for my boy at its first ascension remained up all day.

CHAPTER 27

WAR KITES

LIKE all soldiers, war kites should be trim and martial in appearance. Their uniform may be as brilliant and fanciful as the ingenuity and taste of the builder suggests, always remembering that lightness and strength are essential qualities. An appropriate name or emblem, marked, painted, or pasted on, would serve not only to distinguish the combatants from their more peaceful brother aërostats, but would give to each kite an individuality, and thus allow successful veterans to become famous throughout kitedom. There are but two "arms" to this novel "service," or rather two modes of warfare. The first, *unarmed*, might be compared to the friendly jousts of the knights of old when they met for trials of skill. The second, *armed*, is more like the mortal combat where but one survives.

Unarmed War Kite

The usual form of the unarmed fighting kite is that of the ordinary bow kite. It should be made about two and one-half feet high. Base of bow, fourteen inches below top of spine or centre-stick, and twenty-seven inches broad. Cover the frame with paper cambric. Make the tail of string, with stripes of colored paper inserted in loops an inch or so apart. A paper tassel at the end will give it a finished look. Ten feet is about the proper length of tail for a kite of this size.

In fighting with this unarmed soldier the object is to capture your opponent's kite by entangling its tail in your own string. To do this you must make your kite dart under the twine of your enemy. As soon as it darts let out string rapidly enough to keep your fighter under control, and at the same time allow it to fall to the rear of the other kite. Having accomplished this, drop your ball of string and pull in hand over hand, as fast as possible. If your enemy is not very spry and well up in these tactics, this manœuvre will hopelessly entangle his kite-tail on your string. Then, although the battle is half won, a great deal depends upon your superior quickness, skill, and also upon the strength of your twine, which may break, or your victim may escape with the loss of part of its tail. If, however, you are successful in capturing your prisoner you can write on your kite the date of the victory, and the name of the vanquished warrior. The captive must, in all cases, be returned to its proper owner after the latter has signed his name to the record of his defeat written upon your kite. Thus is the successful hero soon covered with the records of his victories, while the unsuccessful fighter carries a bare blank face.

Armed Kites

are of a more relentless and bloodthirsty order than the strategic unarmed warrior. The peculiar mission of these rampant champions of the air is to cut the enemy off from his base of supplies; then with a satisfied wriggle, and a fiendish wag of the tail, this ferocious flyer sails serenely on, while his ruined victim falls helplessly to the earth, or ignominiously hangs himself on some uncongenial tree, where his skeleton will struggle and swing until beaten to pieces by the very element that sustained him in his elevation before his thread of life was cut. In this sport, new to most Northern boys, they will find an exciting and healthy pastime, one that will teach them to think and act quickly, a quality that when acquired may be of infinite service to them in after years.

Armed Kite Fighting

These aëro-nautical cutters might be appropriately named the Scorpion, "Stingerree," Wasp, or Hornet, because they fight with their tails, the sting of the insect being represented on the kite-tail by the razor-like cutters.

The tactics used in these battles of the clouds are just the opposite from those employed in fighting with unarmed kites.

To win the battle you so manœuvre your warrior that its tail sweeps across and cuts the string of your antagonist.

Armed kites are usually made after the pattern of the American six-sided or hexagonal kite. They are two and one-half feet high, covered with paper cambric, or, when economy is no object, with silk.

As a successful warrior looks well after his arms, so should the tail of a war kite receive the most careful attention.

One very popular style of tail is made of strips of bright-colored cloth about one inch wide tied securely in the middle to a strong twine, the tail ending in a fancy tassel.

Another style is made of long narrow strips of white cloth securely sewed together. This tail is not so apt to become knotted or tangled as the first.

How to Make the Knives

The "cutters" to be attached to the tail are made of sharp pieces of broken glass called knives.

From a thick glass bottle, broken off below the neck, chip off pieces. This can be done with the back of a heavy knife blade or a light hammer. The workman cannot be too careful or cautious in breaking or handling the glass, as the least carelessness is sure to result in bad cuts and bloody fingers.

From the slivers or chips of glass select pieces thick on the outside curve, but with a keen sharp inside edge. It may take time, experience, and several bottles to get knives to exactly suit you.

FIG. 27-1

Cutters

How to Make Cutters

Fasten three knives together with wax (**FIG. 27-1**) so that each shall point in a different direction, bind on this three slips of thin wood lengthwise to hold the wax and glass firmly, and cover it neatly with cloth or kid.

A piece of twine looped at each end should pass through the apparatus lengthwise. This, of course, to be put in before the slips are bound together. Excellent cutters can be made of blades from an old penknife.

A much simpler weapon is made with a piece of stout twine one foot long, dipped in glue and rolled in pounded glass until thickly coated with a glistening armor of sharp points. Two of these incorporated in the lower half of the kite's tail will be found to be effective cutters.

Boys participating in this war of kites should always bear in mind the fact that it requires but little skill to cut an unarmed kite, and that there is no honor or glory to be gained in vanquishing a foe who is unable to defend himself.

There are many other attachments, improvements, and amusing appliances that suggest themselves to an enthusiastic kite-flyer.

Kite Clubs

The field is a large one, and the opportunities for originality and ingenuity almost unbounded. If some enthusiastic, energetic boy will take
the initiatory steps, kite clubs might be formed throughout the country with appropriate names, rules, and regulations, which, during
the kite season, would have their meets and tournaments, and award
prizes to the steadiest stander, the highest flyer, and the most original
and unique design besides the prizes awarded at the jousts of the war
kites.

The organization of such clubs would give a new impetus to an
amusement deserving of greater popularity than it has ever attained
in this country.

☜ CHAPTER 28 ☞

SNOWBALL WARFARE

COLD gray clouds have long since usurped the heavens and driven away the white, fleecy summer cumulus; the latter, like the birds, have gone to more congenial climes. For several weeks past heavy overcoats have been in demand.

The rowing season has closed; the baseball bats and lawn tennis rackets are stowed away, and the college boys have settled down to study and in-door gymnasium practice.

In the cities the car and stage drivers swing their arms about and beat their muffled chests in a vain effort to start the blood to circulating in their benumbed fingers. Each passenger, as he reads the morning paper, exhales two streams of mist from his nostrils. The horses puff larger streams of steam and wear chest protectors. Everybody appears unhappy except the school-boy. The latter's cheeks glow with more than usual color and his eyes sparkle as if with inward merriment, for *he knows the signs,* and the dull, leaden sky to him is only a promise of a big snow storm and "lots of fun." The frost king has arrived and introduced jolly old Winter. Every boy knows that no season of the year can boast of more healthy out-door games, brimful of fun and excitement, than winter, and that there is no sport among winter games more exciting and amusing than snowball warfare. The interest and fun of the game is greatly enhanced if there be a fort to capture or defend.

261

How to Build Snow-Forts

All the boys must join in building the fort, selecting the highest point of the play-grounds, or, if the grounds be level, the corner of a wall or fence. Supposing the top of a mound has been selected as the place where the works are to be built, the first thing to do is to make out the plan of the foundation. The dimensions depend upon the number of boys. A circle twelve feet in diameter, or a square with sides of ten feet, will make a fort that will accommodate a company of ten boys. It is better to have the fort too small than too large. The chief engineer must set his men to rolling large snowballs; the smaller boys can commence them and the larger ones take the balls in hand when they have gained in size and become too heavy for the younger boys.

Make these balls of snow as large and dense as possible; then roll them in place upon the lines traced out for the foundation. We will suppose it to be a square. In this case, care must be taken to have the corners of the square opposite the most probable approach of the enemy. This will leave the smallest point possible exposed to the attack, and the inmates of the fort can, without crowding each other, take

FIG. 28-1

Snow-Fort commenced

FIG. 28-2

Snow-Fort finished

good aim at the foe. After the four sides of the square are covered by large snowballs, as in **FIG. 28-1**, all hands must pack the snow about the bottom and fill up each crack and crevice until a solid wall is formed. Then with spades and shovels the walls should be trimmed down to a perpendicular on the inside, but slanting upon the outside, as shown in **FIG. 28-2**. The top of the wall may be two feet broad and the base four feet. When the wall is finished, prepare a mound of snow in the centre of the square for the flag-staff. This mound will be very useful as a reserve supply in case the ammunition gives out. A quantity of snowballs should next be piled up, inside the walls, at the four corners. This done, the fort is ready for its defenders, and it only remains to equip the attacking force.

The building of a fort generally uses up all the snow around it, making it necessary for the besieging party to carry their ammunition with them upon sleds made for that purpose.

The construction of these sleds is very simple, the materials and tools necessary consisting of a flour-barrel, a saw, a hatchet, some shingle nails and an old pine board.

How to Make an Ammunition Sled

To make the sled, begin by knocking the barrel apart, being careful not to split the head-boards, as they will be needed afterward. Pick out the four best staves, as nearly alike in breadth and curve as can be found, and saw two or three of the other staves in halves. Take two of the four staves first selected and nail the half staves across, as shown in **FIG. 28-3**. These must be nailed upon the convex, or outside, of the staves; this will be found impossible unless there is something solid under the point where the nail is to be driven, otherwise the spring of the stave, when struck, will throw the nail out, and your fingers will probably receive the blow from the hammer. To avoid this, place a block, or anything that

FIG. 28-3

Top of Ammunition Sled

FIG. 28-4

*Ammunition Sled
finished*

FIG. 28-5

is firm, under the point where the nail is to be driven, and there will then be found no difficulty in driving the nails home. When this is done you will have the top of your sled as shown in **FIG. 28-3**; on this you will need a box or bed to hold the snowballs; this you can make of two pieces of pine board and two staves, thus: Take a board about the same width as, or a little wider than, a barrel-stave; saw off two pieces equal in length to the width of the sled; set them upon their edges, reversing the top of the sled; place it across the two boards and nail it on securely. Then take two staves and nail them on for side boards, and you have the top portion of your sled finished.

The two staves remaining of the four first selected are for runners. Fit on first one and then the other to the staves of the top. Nail-holes will probably be found near the ends of the staves where the nails were that held the barrel-head in; through these drive nails to fasten your runners; to do this you must rest them upon some support, as was done before; this will hold your sled together, but to make it stronger take four wedge-shaped blocks of wood and slide them in between the runners and the top, as shown in **FIG. 28-4**, and nail these firmly in place from above and below.

If all this has been properly done, you now have made a sled which it will be almost impossible to break; and, with a rope to pull by, one boy can haul snowballs enough for a dozen companions.

How to Make the Shield

The shield is made from the head of a barrel. Lay the barrel-head upon some level surface, so that nails can be driven in without trouble.

From a strip of board half inch thick and two and one-half inches wide saw off two pieces long enough to fasten the parts of the barrel-head together, as you see them in **FIG. 28-5**. Fasten these strips on firmly with shingle nails.

Lay your left arm upon the shield, as shown, mark a place for the arm-strap just in front of elbow, and another for the strap for the hand. From an old trunk-strap, or suitable piece of leather, cut two strips and nail them on your shield at points marked, being careful that the arm-strap is not too tight, as it should be loose enough for the arm to slip in and out with ease. This done, you have a shield behind which you may defy an army of unprotected boys.

Rules of the Game

The rules of warfare governing a snowball battle are as follows: Two commanders, or captains, must be elected. If the forces engaged be very large, each captain may appoint one or two assistants, or lieutenants. These officers, after being elected and appointed, are to give all orders, and should be promptly obeyed by their respective commands. The captains decide, by lot, the choice of position.

In choosing sides, the captain who is commander of the fort has first choice, then the two captains name a boy, alternately, until two-thirds of the boys have been chosen. The defenders of the fort then retire to their stronghold, leaving the boys unchosen to join the attacking army, it being supposed that one-third behind fortifications are equal to two-thirds outside.

Only the attacking party is allowed shields and ammunition sleds.

At least thirty yards from the fort a camp must be established by the outsiders or attacking army, and stakes driven at the four corners to locate the camp. Imaginary lines from stake to stake mark its limits.

Each party will have its national colors, in addition to which the attacking party has a battle-flag which it carries with it in the assault.

The defenders of the fort must see to it that all damages to the fortifications are promptly repaired. Any soldier from the fort who shall be carried off within the limits of the camp becomes a prisoner of war, and cannot leave the camp until rescued by his own comrades.

Any one of the attacking force pulled into the fort becomes a prisoner of war, and must remain in the fort until it is captured.

Prisoners of war cannot be made to fight against their own side, but they may be employed in making snowballs or repairing damages to fortifications.

Any deserter recaptured must suffer the penalty of having his face washed with snow, and being made to work with the prisoners of war.

When the outsiders, or attacking army, can replace the enemy's colors with their battle-flag, the fort is captured and the battle is won by the attacking party; all fighting must then immediately cease.

But if, in a sally, or, by any means, the soldiers of the fort can take the colors of the opposite party from the camp and bring them inside their fortifications, they have not only successfully defended their fort, but have defeated the attacking army; and this ends the battle, with double honors to the brave defenders.

No water-soaked or icy snow-balls are allowed. No honorable boy uses them, and any one caught in the ungentlemanly act of throwing such "soakers" should be forever ruled out of the game.

No blows are allowed to be struck by the hand, or by anything but the regulation snowball, and, of course, no kicking is permitted.

The following sketch of a snow battle in which the author took part when a boy, will give an idea of the excitement and interest of the game:

A Snow Battle

It was a year when the Indian summer had been prolonged into the winter. Christmas had come and gone and a new year begun, but not one flake of snow had fallen on the river bank or neighboring hills.

Such was the condition of things one January morning in a Kentucky town upon the banks of the Ohio River, where myself and some sixty other boys were gathered in a little frame school-house.

We had about made up our minds that old Jack Frost was a humbug, and winter a myth; but when the bell tapped for recess, the first boy out gave a shout which passed from mouth to mouth until it became a universal cheer as we reached the play-grounds, for floating airily down from a dull, leaden, gray sky came hundreds of white snow-flakes!

Winter had come! Jack Frost was no longer a humbug! Before the bell again recalled us to our study the ground was whitened with snow, and the school divided into two opposing armies. That night was a busy one—all hands set to work manufacturing ammunition sleds and shields for the coming battle. It was my fortune to be chosen as one of the garrison of the fort. There was not a boy late next morning—in fact, when the teachers arrived to open the school, they found all the scholars upon the play-grounds, rolling huge snowballs. All night the snow had continued to fall, and it was now quite deep. When we went out at noon a beautifully modelled fort of snowy whiteness stood ready for us, and from a mound in the centre floated the battle-flag.

Our company took their places inside the fortifications.

We could see the enemy gathered around their captain at their camp some two hundred yards distant, their ammunition sleds loaded with well-made snowballs. The lieutenant bore their battle-flag.

Our teachers showed their interest by standing shivering with wet feet in the deep snow to watch the battle. At a blast from a tin horn on rushed the foe! They separated and came in two divisions, approaching us from the left and right.

"Now, boys," cried our captain, "be careful not to throw a ball until they are within range."

Then, calling the pluckiest among us, a flaxen-haired country boy, to his side, he whispered a word or two and pointed to the flag in the enemy's camp. The boy, who had been nicknamed "Daddy" on account of his old-looking face, slipped quietly over the rear wall of the fort, dodged behind a snow-drift and then behind a fence, and was lost to sight. Forward marched the enemy, their battle-flag borne in advance of the party to the right. Their captain was at the head of the division to the left.

Having engaged our attention on the two flanks, where we stood ready to receive them, as they neared us, by a quick and well-executed manœuvre, rushing obliquely toward each other, the two divisions unexpectedly joined, and advanced, shield to shield, with the ammunition sleds in the rear. It was in vain we pelted them with snowballs; on they came, encouraged by a cheer from the teachers and some spectators who by this time had gathered near the school-house.

Three times had our noble captain been tumbled from his perch upon the mound in the centre of the fort, when another burst of applause from the spectators announced some new development, and as we looked, we could see "Daddy" with the colors of the enemy's camp in his arms, his tow hair flying in the wind as he ran for dear life.

In an instant the line of the enemy was all in confusion; some ran to head off "Daddy," while others in their excitement stood and shouted. It was our turn now, and we pelted their broken ranks with snow until they looked like animated snow-men. Another shout, and we looked around to find our captain down and the hands of one of the besieging party almost upon our flag. It was the work of a second to pitch the intruder upon his back outside the fort. Then came the tug of war. A rush was made to capture our standard, several of our boys were pulled out of the fort and taken prisoners, and the capture of the fort seemed inevitable. Again and again a number of the enemy, among whom was their color-bearer, gained the top of our breastworks, and again and again were they tumbled off amid a shower of snowballs that forced them to retire to gain breath and clear their eyes from the snow. Once their lieutenant, with the red-bordered battle-flag, had actually succeeded in reaching the mound upon which stood our colors, when a combined attack that nearly resulted in his being made prisoner drove him from the fort to gather strength for another rush. "Daddy" was now a prisoner, and the recaptured flag again floated over the enemy's camp, when the school-bell called us, fresh and glowing with exercise and healthful excitement, to our lessons. The battle was left undecided, but our fort was soon captured by a force stronger than any our companions were able to bring against it, for a warm south wind sprang up from the lowlands down the river, and our fortification quickly yielded to its insidious attack, and the snow campaign was over.

How to Bind a Prisoner Without a Cord

A gentleman who was much interested in the foregoing description of snowball warfare sends a sketch of the manner he and his playmates used to bind their prisoners taken in snow battles. The captive was taken to a post or smooth-trunked sapling and compelled to put his arms and legs around it as if he were about to climb. The right leg crossed the left leg, and the toe of the right shoe was pushed behind the post or tree trunk in the position shown by the illustration. After taking this position the prisoner was gently pushed down into a sitting position. It is next to impossible for a person so fixed to arise without help. The toe of the left shoe binds the right leg; the toe of the right shoe binds the post, and the arms can be only used to hold on by. When a friend reaches the captive he takes him by the arms and lifts him up. As soon as the prisoner assumes an upright position he can free himself without difficulty.

FIG. 28-6

A Prisoner of War

Company Rest

The same gentleman who sent the above ingenious device also tells of some funny manœuvres the boys used to go through. For instance, during a lull in the battle, the commander would call out "Company rest!" One man then assumed a stooping position; the next man sat on the right knee of the first man; a third man would sit upon the right knee of the second man and so on until a circle was formed, each fellow sitting in some other fellow's lap and yet no one sitting upon anything else. "Thus," says the correspondent, "we all were enabled to sit down without using the damp snow for a camp stool."

FIG. 28-7

A Snow-House Finished

CHAPTER 29

SNOW STATUARY

THE statuary may be of various kinds. It is very seldom that pigs are sculptured in marble or cast in bronze, and it would be well to make some of snow, so as to have statues not likely to be found elsewhere. An oblong mass of snow forms the body (**FIG. 29-1**); the legs, nose, and ears are made of sticks surrounded by

FIG. 29-1

Making the Pig

snow, and a bit of rope nicely curled will make a very good tail. The various parts can be shaped and carved according to the skill of the young artist. A number of pigs, of different sizes, will give a lively and social air to the yard of a snow-house. **FIG. 29-2** shows a finished pig.

A statue of a Frenchman in an ulster is also rather uncommon, and is not hard to make. The foundation of the body, head, and legs consists of several large snowballs, as seen in **FIG. 29-3**, and the arms are made

FIG. 29-2

A Snow Pig

of smaller balls stuck on two sticks, which are inserted in the body at proper angles. When the whole figure has been "blocked out," as the artists say, it must be carved, with broad wooden knives or shingles, into the proper shape, as shown in **FIG. 29-4**. The moustache should be made of icicles, which may be stuck in the face.

Arctic owls, which are very large and white, can also be made of snow, in the manner shown in the adjoining picture. These figures can be placed on snow pedestals if they are small, but if they are monster owls, like those in the illustrations (**FIGS. 29-5** and **29-6**), they must be placed upon the ground. In either position, if they are fashioned properly, they will look very wise and respectable.

When the snow is too dry to make a snowball it cannot be used to make statuary, but after a slight thaw or a fresh fall of snow it readily adheres upon a slight

FIG. 29-3

Making "Frenchy"

pressure, and can be formed or fashioned in almost any shape.

Many curious objects and figures may be carved out of solidly packed balls of snow. A lawn covered with a number of large snow figures presents a most grotesque appearance, and is sure to attract the attention of all passers-by. With practice not a little skill may be acquired by the young sculptor, and if the statuary be made of large proportions, they will sometimes last for weeks after the snow has disappeared from the ground and house-tops.

FIG. 29-4

Frency in his Ulster

FIG. 29-5

Carving the Owl

FIG. 29-6

An Arctic Owl

CHAPTER 30

SLEDS
CHAIR-SLEIGHS
AND SNOW-SHOES

THE construction of one of the simplest sleds is shown by **FIG. 30-1**; it consists of nothing more nor less than three pieces of board nailed upon two barrel-staves. The barrel-stave sled possesses the advantage of being so simple in design that a child might make one, and although this primitive sled can lay claim to neither grace nor beauty, it will be found useful in a variety of ways; it may be used for coasting, or for transporting loads of snow when building snow houses, forts or figures. If, instead of the long top board, a kitchen chair be fitted on, as shown in **FIG. 30-2**,

FIG. 30-1

Barrel-stave Sled

A Chair-Sleigh

FIG. 30-2

A Chair-Sleigh

will be had. It is necessary to nail on four L-shaped blocks at a proper distance apart on the cross board to hold the chair in place (**FIG. 30-2**). Any boy who is fortunate enough to have a mother or sister who takes sufficient interest, and has the time to accompany him on his skating trips, will find a chair-sleigh quite a handy thing to possess, and when he moves from

FIG. 30-3

FIG. 30-4

one part of the ice to a distant portion of the pond or river he can skate behind the sleigh with his hands upon the back of the chair, and push his lady friend rapidly over the ice, adding much to her enjoyment as well as his own.

The cumbersome wooden kitchen chair is heavy to carry if the skating pond be far from home, but a

Folding Chair-Sleigh

may be made from a few sticks and pieces of leather for hinges. This chair is made upon the same principle as the one described in the chapter devoted to, "How to Camp Out." **FIGS. 30-3** and **30-4** show all the parts in detail as they would look before being joined together. The seat may be made of a piece of carpet, canvas, or any strong material, the hinges of leather. **FIG. 30-5** shows the chair after it has been put together. The runners consist of skates, which may be strapped on or taken off at pleasure, without injuring the skates in the least. If the chair is to be carried it can be folded up. When the chair frame is lifted the forked sticks that support it will slip from the notches in the side bars and fall on to the runner bars; the chair frame can then be let down and the whole frame-work will form a flat, compact mass (**FIG. 30-6**), that can be easily carried by quite a small boy. By using light sticks, regular metal hinges, and a prettily worked cloth for the seat, a very light and beautiful chair-sleigh can be made that, with the skates removed, will make an ornamental parlor chair for summer, and when the ice again covers the surface of the water, it will be only necessary to strap on the skates, and the easy chair becomes transformed into a chair-sleigh, to be pushed about over the glittering ice wherever its occupant may direct or the whim of the boy who forms the motive power may take him.

FIG. 30-5

Folding Chair-Sleigh Ready for Use

The Toboggan

This sled, familiar to all who visit Canada or the Provinces during the winter months, is more like a mammoth snow-shoe than the ordinary sled, sleigh or jumper that we are accustomed to see. It is suitable for the deep snow and heavy drifts of the northern countries, where the runners of a common sleigh would be liable to break through the crust and bury themselves, thus imped-

FIG. 30-6

Folded Up

ing, if not altogether stopping, the vehicle. The toboggan presents a broad, smooth bottom to the snow, and glides over the crust.

To make one of these sleds you must procure two pieces of quarter-inch pine lumber eight or ten feet long and one foot wide. Place the two boards side by side and join them together by the means of round cross sticks; the latter are bound to the bottom board by thongs; the

FIG. 30-7

The Toboggan

thongs pass through holes in the bottom boards on each side of the cross stick, and are made fast by a series of "hammock hitches" (see page 10, and **FIG. 1-10**, E). Where the thongs pass underneath the bottom board grooves are cut deep enough to prevent the cord from projecting; the grooves are quite necessary, for if the cords were allowed to project beyond the surface of the boards they would not only impede the progress of the toboggan, but the friction would soon wear out the thongs and the sled would come apart. On top of the cross sticks two side bars are lashed; the front ends of the board are then curled over and held in position by two thongs made fast to the ends. **FIG. 30-7** shows a finished toboggan drawn from one manufactured by the Indians in Canada.

Snow-Shoes or Skates

The Norwegian ski is a snow-shoe, or rather a snow-skate, nine feet long, used by the Norwegians to glide down the mountains or hillsides when the latter are covered with snow.

Great fun can be had with a pair of snow-shoes made on the same principle as the Norwegian skate shoe, and it is little trouble to manufacture a pair from two barrel staves.

FIG. 30-8

Top and Side View of Barre-Stave Skate

After selecting a couple of straight-grained staves, score one end of each stave with grooves cut in the wood either with your knife or a small gouge, as shown by the lines at A, **FIG. 30-8**. Smear the end thickly with grease and hold it near a hot fire until you find that it can be bent into the form shown by the diagram (**FIG. 30-8**); bind it in position by a cord and let it remain so until the wood retains the curve imparted. Make two blocks, each one inch broad and high enough to fit under the heels of your shoes; fasten the blocks on to the snow-skates by screws (C, **FIG. 30-8**); at a proper distance in front of the block fasten two straps securely (B, **FIG. 30-8**). By slipping the toes of your shoes through the straps and allowing the hollow of the foot to rest over the blocks C, C, so that the heels of your shoes bear against the blocks, you can keep the shoes on your feet, and, with the aid of a stick to steer by, go sliding down the coasting hill among the sleds and jumpers, creating as much fun for the others in your first attempts as you do for yourself; but with practice skill can be acquired in the use of snow-skates.

FIG. 30-9

Notes on Snow-Shoes

Away out in Wyoming some of our cowboy friends had great fun with the barrel-stave sleds described on page 263. They did not use them for ammunition sleds to carry snow-balls, but as toboggans. I am informed by one of the "boys," Mr. Dan Smith, that near his ranch, which is located at the foothills of the Big Horn Mountains, there is a very tall and steep-sided hill or mountain, the apex of which is scarcely large enough for a man to stand on, and is reached by a zigzag walk.

Early in the spring, after the first thaw had frozen, making a thick crust on the snow, Mr. Smith built him a barrel-stave sled, climbed to the top of the mountain with his wooden steed, and shot down the precipitous side. Down, down he went, like the wind! clearing slight hollows with a bound through the air, which excited the wildest enthusiasms among the cowboys, Indians, and half-breeds, and it was not long before there was not a barrel left in all the region around; and all day long, as long as the crust lasted, these grown-up boys flew down the mountain side amid shouts and laughter on the barrel-stave sleds described in Chapter 28.

Barrel-stave Show-shoe

Each barrel-stave snow-shoe consists of two staves, set just far enough apart to allow the sole of an old shoe to rest between. (**FIG. 30-9**). The staves are joined together by cross-pieces near each end, arranged as shown in the diagram.

FIG. 30-10

FIG. 30-11

From a pair of old boots or shoes, much too large for the expectant show-shoer, a pair of rude slippers are made by the aid of a sharp knife (**FIG. 30-10**). This show or slipper is screwed firmly to the second cross-stick, as shown in **FIG. 30-9**, the back part of the slipper is allowed to rest upon and is fastened to the net-work, made of clothes-line, or any other small rope or heavy twine. The rope is strung through holes in the sides of the staves, which have been bored with a red-hot iron.

The part where the line comes upon the under part of the shoe can be grooved with the same hot iron, so that the rope will not project beyond the stave and impede the movements of the snow-shoer in sliding or coasting down inclines.

Lace the shoes on the feet, after the manner shown in the diagram (**FIG. 30-11**), and you have a pair of very serviceable crusting shoes, that is, shoes to use when a crust has formed over the surface of a deep snow which is not sufficient strength to prevent the unprotected shoe from crushing through at each step, but will bear a snow-shoer safely, on account of his weight being distributed over a large space (see illustration).

These shoes can also be used in travelling over boggy ground in the summer.

Again the author finds that the most difficult part of such a book as this is the end, for after he has gone over the seasons in detail as he did when a boy, it is hard to lay down the pen and again plunge into the busy world along with other old boys the tops of whose heads begin to resemble what the lads in Kentucky called "alleys," a sort of flesh-colored marble or "Meg" with faint blue veins on it, very hard and very shiny.

FIG. 30-12

CHAPTER 31

THE WINGED SKATERS AND HOW TO MAKE THE WINGS

SKIMMING over the glassy surface of an ice-bound river or pond, propelled by the wintry blast blowing against artificial wings of cloth, is but a degree removed from flying. The friction of your skate runners upon the ice is so slight that it is not difficult to imagine that you have left the earth and are soaring in mid-air.

Every boy who has had any skating experience knows what hard work it is to skate against a stiff wind, and almost all who ever fastened skates to their feet must have enjoyed the luxury of sailing over the ice before the wind with a spread coat or open umbrella doing duty as a sail.

For some time back people in widely separated parts of the world have made more or less successful attempts at transforming themselves into animated ice-yachts, and in Canada, Norway, and other cold countries, men with sails rigged on their backs or shoulders have "tacked," "come about," and "luffed" themselves in a novel and highly entertaining style, but lately, for some reason or other, this sport has been allowed to almost die out, and we are now indebted to two or three writers for reintroducing skate-sailing to the public with original suggestions and improvements. Mr. Charles L. Norton, editor of *The American Canoeist*, was, I believe, the first to call the attention of the public in general, and the boys particularly, to this delightful sport. In an article published in the *St. Nicholas Magazine*, entitled "Every Boy his Own

Ice-Boat," Mr. Norton describes a new and original device, consisting of a double sail, which is so simple in construction, and yet so strong, light, and easy to manage, that it is sure to become a favorite rig with the boys, both large and small.

In another article entitled "White Wings," which appeared in *Harper's Weekly*, the same author describes a number of queer sails used by different people. Following in the footsteps of Mr. Norton, and adding to our information on this subject, comes T. F. Hammer with an interesting article published in the *Century Magazine*, in which this gentleman gives some personal experience as a winged skater and a detailed description of the Danish skate-sail.

Among the many reasons given by skate-sailors why this new and highly exhilarating pastime should come into general favor are these: skate-sailing can be practised and enjoyed on ice too rough for ordinary skating, and a light fall of snow that ruins the ice for the common skater improves it for the winged yachtsman.

Salt-water ice that is too soft for one to enjoy a skate upon affords a better foothold than smooth, hard, fresh-water ice, and is preferable on that account. Wherever you can skate there you may sail, and when the skating proper is ruined, it often happens that the qualities of the ice are improved for sailing. There is no record of a serious accident happening to any skate-sailor, although one may attain, literally, the speed of the wind, the higher the rate of speed the less danger there appears to be, for in failing a person will strike the ice at such an angle that he is merely sent sliding over the surface, and little or no damage is done.

Bat Wings

After procuring a suitable piece of cloth, spread it out upon the floor and tack it there, then spread yourself out on the cloth with your arms extended at right angles to your body, and your feet spread apart. While in that position, have some one mark on the cloth the points where the crown of your head, your wrists, and ankles come. With a chalk or pencil connect these points by lines, and, allowing for the hem, cut the sail out according to the pattern made.

Turn the edges over and make a strong broad hem all around the sail, sew in straps or bands at the ankle, waist, wrists, and head. When the sail is to be used, adjust the head-band around the forehead, fasten the waist, wrist, and ankle straps, and the ship is rigged. By spreading the arms, the sail is set; when the arms are folded the sail is furled. It would become exceedingly tiresome to hold the arms outstretched from the sides for any length of time without support; to obviate this, a stick may be carried, which, when thrust behind the back, will make a support for the hands as they grasp it near the ends. The man-bat steers with his feet, using his legs and arms for sheet-lines. Skaters rigged up in this novel style present a most grotesque appearance as they flap their wings about in going through various evolutions.

The Norton Rig

is a double sail, and might be called a schooner rig. It is in many respects superior to the somewhat cumbersome single sails, the chief advantage being the fact that the crew can see in every direction, and thus avoid running foul of any other craft or skater. Another improvement is the double main spar which, without increasing the weight, affords a stronger support for the cross pieces, or fore and main masts. The main spar may be made of spruce pine or bamboo. Cane fishing-poles are inexpensive, and can probably be readily obtained by most boys. Select two pieces, each about ten feet long, and bind the butt or large end of one to the small end of the other; lash the other ends firmly together in like manner, so that the two poles will lay side by side firmly bound at each end.

For the fore and main masts or cross yards, Mr. Norton recommends bamboo, five-eighths of an inch in diameter, but American cane will also answer for that purpose. Pick out two pieces five-eighths of an inch in diameter at the smallest ends, and let each be four feet six inches long. Near the ends of the cross yards fasten metal buttons or knobs, and fasten similar knobs near the ends of the main spar. Make a small cleat for the middle of each cross spar (A, **FIG. 31-1**) and lash it firmly on.

Make the sails of the heaviest cotton sheeting, if it can be procured; if not, take ordinary sheeting and double it, or what cloth you can procure. Mark out the sails, making allowance for the hem, and let them measure four feet across the diagonal after the hem has been turned down; bind the sails with strong tape, and see that the corners particularly are made very strong. Sew to the "clews" or corners small metal rings, or loops of strong cord, to fasten on the buttons at the ends of the spars.

FIG. 31-1

The Norton Rig

Attach the sails to the cross spars by slipping the rings at the clews over the buttons at each end of the spars. Spring the main spar apart and slip the cleats of the cross spar between the two pieces, so that they fit as shown by **FIG. 31-1**. Fasten the outside clews to the buttons on the ends of the main spar and bind the two inside clews tightly together with a cord as shown in the diagram, and you are all ready to give the novel device a trial. Go to the nearest sheet of ice, put on your skates, and after seeing that they are securely fastened, take up the sails and let yourself go before the wind, steering with your feet. After practising awhile you can learn to tack, and go through all the manœuvres of a regular sail-boat.

A most beautiful "rig" is described by Mr. Norton, in which the main spar consists of four pieces of bamboo joined at the middle by brass fishing-rod ferrules. Brass tips are used for holding the small ends of the bamboo together at the ends of the main spar. This rig can be taken apart like a jointed fishing-rod, and, like it, put in a comparatively small case, occupying not much more space when the sails are rolled up than an old-fashioned cotton umbrella. Sails may be made of fancy striped cloth and brilliantly colored penants rigged to their corners; combine this with a suitable uniform, and the winged skater will present a most striking and dashing appearance as he goes flying over the ice.

The Norwegian Rig

This is a very simple sail to make, as may be seen by referring to **FIG. 31-2**. The spars can be made of the same material as the ones described

for the Norton rig. The Norwegian rig requires a crew of two, and in this particular differs from all the rest. The man at the bow grasps the main spar with one hand just behind the fore cross yard, and with the other hand takes hold of the main spar behind him; the helmsman must stand at the stern or "aft" end of the sail, so that he can see to steer. The man in front must hold on and trust to Providence and the steersman. This is rather an awkward rig, but it has the advantage of carrying two instead of one, and is consequently in favor with people who like sociability.

FIG. 31-2

The Norweigan Rig

The Danish Rig

consists of a mainmast and topmast. The latter can be let down when required. The diagram (**FIG. 31-3**) is made of dimensions suitable for a good-sized boy. The straps near the bottom of the topmast are for the purpose of binding the sail to the back of the crew, like a knapsack. The hand-sticks are only attached to the lower corners of the sails, the other ends are held by the crew, crossed and used as sheet-lines are in an

FIG. 31-3

The Danish Rig

ordinary sail-boat. The spars may all be made of spruce, pine, cedar, bamboo, or Southern cane, and the sail of heavy cotton sheeting or strong cotton duck, of double thickness at the clews. In experimenting with this rig, it is best to choose a day when there is only a moderate wind, for the sail being bound to your body cannot be cast aside by simply letting go.

The mainsail and topsail are all of one piece of cloth. The topmast is fastened to the middle of the shoulder yard by a leather strap passing around the yard. The topmast is held in place by the wind blowing it against the head of the crew. By running a little into the wind the topsail will fall back and leave only the mainsail up, or if you loosen the cross knot at the upper part of the topmast you can roll the topsail down to the reefing points and lash it there. The steering is done with the feet of the crew. To learn to sail this or any other craft practice is needed. You might as well try to learn to swim from reading a book as to expect to become an expert sailor without going to sea.

FIG. 31-4

The English Rig

The English Rig

consists of a mast and two spars (**FIG. 31-4**); the bottom of the mast rests in straps fastened to one leg of the crew, who supports the sail by placing one arm around the mast, holding on to the top spar with the other hand. This makes quite a pretty craft, though, like the Danish rig, the sail must be bound to the crew, which always appears objectionable from the fact that in case of accident there must be more danger of breaking the spars or tearing the sail than there is where the whole thing can be dropped in an instant. The English rig is on something of the same principle as

The Cape Vincent Rig

which consists of a long spar and a sprit, the spar being in some cases twelve or fifteen feet in length; one seven feet long will make a sail large enough for a boy. The sprit is fastened at the bottom securely to the sail, and fits on to the main spar with a crotch, fork, or jaw. The sail being cut in the right shape and proper proportions, and made fast to the

long spar and to the end of the sprit, as soon as the latter is forced into place it will stretch the sail out flat, as in **FIG. 31-5**. A boy with one of these rigs on his shoulder makes a very rakish-looking craft. The spar is carried "as a soldier carries his rifle"—on the shoulder; the sprit, or

FIG. 31-5

The Cape Vincent Rig

small cross spar, is allowed to rest against the crew's back. According to one writer, who is supposed to have had experience, this rakish craft will not in the least belie its looks. In speaking of it he says: "I should say that on good, smooth ice, with a twenty-five or thirty-mile wind, they went at the rate of eighty or *one hundred miles an hour*." This sounds like an exaggeration, but when we remember that a good ice-yacht, well handled, can make a mile a minute or more, travelling much faster than the wind itself, the statement of the enthusiastic advocate of the Cape Vincent rig does not appear so improbable. In speaking of the speed attained by regular ice-yachts, Mr. Norton says:

"There is no apparent reason why a skate-sailor should not attain a like speed. Other things being equal, he has certain advantages over the ice-yacht. His steering gear is absolutely perfect, assuming, of course, that he is a thoroughly confident skater, and it is in intimate sympathy with the trim of his sail. This nice adjustment between rudder and sails is an important point. Again, there is no rigidity about the rig. Everything sways and gives under changing conditions of wind, and experience soon endows the skater with an instinct which teaches him to trim his sail so as to make every ounce of air-pressure tell to the best advantage."

A Country Rig

The two forked sticks from which the framework of this sail is made must necessarily be nearly of the same dimensions. After their ends have been firmly lashed together, as shown by **FIG. 31-6**, a sail made of an old piece of carpet, awning, hay-cover, or any cloth that is strong enough or can be made strong enough by doubling, may be lashed on at the four prongs of the forks. This rig will convey a crew of two over the ice with as much speed as the more elaborate Norwegian sail (**FIG. 31-2**). The country sail may not be handsome, but it possesses the advantage of being easily constructed and costing little or nothing, except the work of cutting and trimming the spars and sail.

FIG. 31-6

The Colony Rig